THE MODERN AMBASSADOR

The Challenge and the Search

THE INSTITUTE FOR THE STUDY OF DIPLOMACY concentrates on the *processes* of conducting foreign relations abroad, in the belief that diplomatic skills can be taught or improved and that the case study method is useful to that end. The Institute emphasizes in its publications program such practical aspects of diplomacy as reporting, analysis, policy recommendation, negotiation, mediation, conciliation, conference diplomacy, representation, consular affairs, and the promotion of business by diplomats as well as domestic influences on the conduct of American diplomacy. Working in association with other segments of Georgetown University, with government officials, and other area academic institutions, the Institute also conducts a program of research, panels, conferences, and lectures. An Associates Program enables experienced practitioners of international relations to conduct individual research while sharing their firsthand experience with the university community.

Inquiries should be addressed to:

The Honorable Ellsworth Bunker
Institute for the Study of Diplomacy
School of Foreign Service
Georgetown University
Washington, D.C. 20057
(202) 625-3784

THE MODERN AMBASSADOR

The Challenge and the Search

Edited by Martin F. Herz

Foreword by Peter F. Krogh

Introduction by Ellsworth Bunker

**INSTITUTE FOR THE STUDY OF DIPLOMACY
EDMUND A. WALSH SCHOOL OF FOREIGN SERVICE
GEORGETOWN UNIVERSITY**

Library of Congress Cataloging in Publication Data
Main entry under title:

The Modern ambassador.

  Includes bibliographical references.
  1. Ambassadors—United States.   2. Ambassadors.
I. Herz, Martin Florian, 1917–   II. Georgetown
University.   Institute for the Study of Diplomacy.
JX1706.A59M55 1983   353.008′92   83-12853
ISBN 0-934742-26-X
ISBN 0-934742-25-1 (pbk.)

Printed in the United States of America

Institute for the Study of Diplomacy
School of Foreign Service
Georgetown University
Washington, DC 20057

About This Monograph

The title of "Ambassador" is coveted—and misunderstood. The word, depending on the circumstances, conjures up images of elegantly-dressed people under crystal chandeliers or devilishly clever (yet effete) foreigners scheming to outwit each other. Too seldom are the questions of the role and the choice of the real-life ambassadors—the official representatives of one country to another—seriously addressed. To address them is the purpose of this monograph.

How relevant is the task of an ambassador to the requirements of the modern world? Are diplomatic skill and experience still helpful to a country's foreign relations? Just what does an ambassador do today? Who should be an ambassador? These are all legitimate questions.

Once again there is focus on the issue of the qualifications and selection of ambassadors—in the press, in the Congress, and in the foreign affairs community. New approaches are being suggested to insure a higher quality of ambassador, whether from private life or from the Foreign Service.

As a contribution to that discussion, this monograph presents a variety of factual data and points of view on the role and selection of ambassadors, including the views of both Americans and non-Americans who have served in that position. The conflicting sides of the perennial debate about the best source for ambassadorial talent are presented, with views from the advocates of non-career as well as career appointments.

The Institute for the Study of Diplomacy is grateful to the many who have contributed essays and comments and to the copyright holders who have permitted us to reprint significant previous work on this subject. The Institute also thanks the Una Chapman Cox Foundation for its generous grant to support the production and promotion of this work.

Foreword

Peter F. Krogh

Dean, School of Foreign Service, Georgetown University

This publication is the latest in a series issued by the Institute for the Study of Diplomacy, dealing with "operational" aspects of foreign relations. It is honestly controversial as befits the presentation and discussion of subjects that are in contention. The reading of it should contribute to a better understanding of the functions of modern ambassadors and where one should search for the best people to fill such positions. The monograph ranges beyond the question of the choice of ambassadors to address the challenge of the new environment, which has in important ways modified—some even believe it has rendered obsolete—the traditional role of ambassadors. I am pleased that the editor, Ambassador Martin F. Herz, who has himself written extensively on the subject, has cast the net widely for contributions of greatly varied points of view.

The School of Foreign Service of Georgetown University is the largest school in the world devoted exclusively to the training of professionals in the field of foreign relations broadly defined. Our function is to prepare future practitioners and leaders in all activities that involve relations with foreign countries—government, business, banking, communications, international organizations, foundations, etc. In so far as future diplomats are concerned, our mission is to train persons to take on growing responsibilities, including eventually those of ambassador, regardless of whether such a position is attained through the career service or through experience in other professional activities that are germane to the conduct of international relations.

Because we define the term "professional" to include persons with backgrounds outside the career diplomatic service that qualify them for consideration and appointment to ambassadorial positions, we certainly are not neutral on the question of whether ambassadors should be professionals. But we take no position on the question of "career versus non-career" beyond advising that the position should go to professionals and that professionals can be found in many places.

It is a peculiarity of American politics that new administrations frequently distrust the professionals in foreign affairs whom they have inherited to carry forward the new policies that they wish to institute. This is just as true of Democrats as of Republicans. It was thus not out of the ordinary that when the Eisenhower Administration took over in 1953, it should have done so with profound reservations about the professionals in the State Department and the Foreign Service. The election campaign had involved charges of "softness" toward communism on the part of the incumbent administration and suspicions of incompetence or even treasonable activity that might explain the reverses the United States had suffered, especially in the Far East. Thus John Foster Dulles asked State Department civil and Foreign Service personnel to display not only loyalty but "positive loyalty" toward the new administration. It would in my opinion be quite wrong to attribute this suspiciousness toward the diplomatic professionals some thirty years ago solely to the influence of Senator Joseph McCarthy. It was McCarthy who inspired the purges of our diplomats under Dulles—but the distrust of them by the incoming administration was not very different from that displayed by other administrations. It was due to the belief, very simply, that professionals who had loyally implemented the foreign policy of the predecessor administration could not possibly find it in their hearts to support a different policy. Yet that is precisely what career officers do—they accept the new dispensation and serve their new master as a matter of course. And nobody finds it remarkable that the foreign policy personnel of Great Britain, France, Germany and Japan, to mention only a few, do the same when there is a change of administration and foreign policy orientation in those countries.

When the Eisenhower administration was replaced by that of John F. Kennedy, the new team took it for granted that especially top career professionals could not possibly understand and loyally implement new policy approaches. Chester Bowles, appointed Undersecretary of State in 1961, described the prevailing attitude of the new administration as follows [in his book, *Promises to Keep*, page 315]:

"The career officers who had risen most quickly in the State Department arena during the 1950s and who now had the most important missions abroad had, with notable exceptions, largely accepted the Dulles perspective of a world in which the good guys (the Americans) and the bad guys (the Soviets) would remain locked in combat for the foreseeable future. Normally, these men would expect to continue as ambassadors, no matter what the changes in an administration. However, I believed it essential that we distinguish between those who could be expected conscientiously to carry out the policies of the Kennedy administration and those who were so committed to the old policies that they could not be expected to change direction.''

It is not my purpose to examine here whether the views held by Mr. Bowles and the Kennedy administration were correct—we must simply note that they existed and that they have their parallels in the administrations of predecessors and successors right up to the present. Nor is it my purpose to examine whether the screening of professionals that was then undertaken tended to "politicize" the Foreign Service by putting simplistic labels ("thinks like us" and "thinks like our predecessors") on individuals. I suppose it is natural that every new government should seek, among the professionals it inherits and among people outside, individuals who it believes will be particularly attuned to the new policy approaches and with whom it thus feels especially comfortable. This is particularly appropriate with regard to policy-making positions. The reverse side of the situation, however, is that many dedicated supporters of a past foreign policy are often not given an opportunity to show that they can serve a new policy with equal effectiveness. While most other countries have found their bureaucracies quite adaptable, in the United States it usually takes a long time before incoming administrations discover that most professionals do not wear ideological blinders.

It may be that the changes in American foreign policy between one administration and another are more far-reaching and more turbulent than the changes in other countries, but there are some who prefer to think that there really is a remarkable amount of consistency and continuity in the basic elements of American foreign policy and that in retrospect even those who entered office with ideas of sweeping change did not really change substance so much as symbols and images. Under these circumstances there is a question whether any new administration isn't really best served by a core of people who assure a minimum of continuity and who constitute a repository of lessons learned from past mistakes. As one Undersecretary of State exhorted the Foreign Service [Nicholas

Katzenbach on October 27, 1966]: "The proof of a true professional, no matter how experienced, is that he never loses a sense of skepticism, a grain of suspicion, and a germ of doubt." Of course it is natural that such persons would at first seem antipathetic to political leaders who want to change the world, at least until they find that changing the world takes a little longer than they had expected.

As one looks over the record of American diplomatic appointments, the remarkable thing is that the Foreign Relations Committee has so rarely looked into the fitness of individual appointees. The result is that the record in regard to the selection of ambassadors is a mixed one. The range is all the way from scandalous to extraordinarily distinguished. Among the distinguished non-career appointees who come to mind are W. Averell Harriman, David K. E. Bruce, and our own Ellsworth Bunker. Among career officers perhaps the best known since World War II have been Loy W. Henderson, Jefferson Caffery, George V. Allen, and Llewellyn E. Thompson. Of course there are many other outstanding ambassadors who could be mentioned in both categories. To analyze their performance would have burst the bounds of this monograph, but the existence of such giants should be noted. I think nobody would deny that there have also been pygmies, in both categories. Obviously it would be good to have more of the former kind and less of the latter. It is my hope that this little publication will contribute to making the search for the right ones easier.

No one can possibly deny that the President has full discretion with regard to the ambassadorial nominations that he sends to the Senate. Yet there is a growing awareness that all is not well in the methods of screening and selection that have been employed in the past. It is the premise of this publication that the search for new principles and procedures may turn out to be a public service and that the establishment of standards and criteria for ambassadorial appointments, and a mechanism encouraging adherence to them, would have beneficial results for our country's diplomacy.

Contents

Introduction

Ellsworth Bunker

Chairman, Institute for the Study of Diplomacy

While I am not in the habit of volunteering for hazardous assignments, I also do not believe one should refuse an assignment just because it is dangerous or difficult; and so I have yielded to the editor's summons to introduce this monograph. I even do so with some pleasure—despite the hazards of flying brickbats that it entails—because I believe that having served in the field of both business and diplomacy over a considerable period of time, I may be able to render some service in addressing various misperceptions that persist about the role and qualifications of the modern ambassador.

To launch the discussion I would like to say a few words on the question of the relevance of the ambassador to the diplomatic process and whether the position has been rendered obsolete by modern technology. I am bemused by the currency which the notion has achieved that rapid electronic communications or roving emissaries have reduced the resident ambassador's role to that of messenger— or rendered it altogether unnecessary. From my own experience the opposite is often the case in both bilateral and multilateral diplomacy.

Instant communication does not produce instant understanding, let alone instant agreement. Successful shuttle diplomacy among several countries or parties and negotiations in multilateral organizations depend on the effectiveness of resident ambassadors so long as the nation state remains the basis of political decisions. Therefore on-the-spot knowledge and assessment assume perhaps even greater importance in an era of rapid communication, to reduce both misunderstanding and distortion.

Moreover, because communications are now so fast, it is more feasible than it used to be for an ambassador to be part of the policy-formulating process. Naturally, he does not wait to be invited to participate. If he has well-founded recommendations on how his instructions should be drafted, he can insert them at the right time and the right place—something that was quite impossible in the

1

days of sailing ships or even steamships. If the man on the spot says to Washington, "If you do it this way it will work, but if you do it that way it won't," very often he will have his way, precisely because rapid telecommunications allow him to argue his case in timely fashion. Many an ambassador can shape and has shaped policy in this manner.

What are the qualities most needed in an ambassador, given the prior assumption that he (or she) enjoys the confidence of the President? Many of the contributions printed in this symposium set forth different factors, always with excellent justification. My own view is that a combination is needed of character, knowledge of foreign countries, and seasoning in diplomatic skills. I put character first, even though this requirement exists in any profession, because there is a belief in some quarters that a successful ambassador must be exceptionally clever, perhaps even devious. I think the statement that an ambassador is "an honest man sent abroad to lie for his country" has done a great deal of mischief, and it is usually not known or remembered that the man who coined that witticism (Sir Francis Wotton) ruined his career with it. In my own experience I have found that the man or woman whose chief attribute is to think rings around everyone else usually produces less useful results than the one who comes across as competent, empathic, honest, fair and trustworthy.

Where, then, are people with the requisite qualifications to be found? Both inside and outside the career service, though they may be much harder to identify outside. By an odd turn of fate it has been my lot to be both a "political appointee" ambassador and a Foreign Service officer. I did not come up through the ranks but had the FSO status conferred upon me, rather to my surprise, when I had served twenty years at chief of mission rank. This little known aspect of the Foreign Service Act is not, apparently, something that is invoked very often, for reportedly there is no other political appointee ambassador who similarly joined the Foreign Service ranks through sheer longevity.

However, my claim to non-partisanship on the "career vs. non-career" issue really rests on other grounds. My definition of a professional diplomat is someone who has had a succession of diplomatic appointments, usually of increasing importance, in which one acquires more and more experience. Combined with presumed natural aptitudes and appropriate earlier education, this experience then assures that the "professional" will perform in a predictable, dependable, and wise way in positions of special delicacy and responsibility.

It is fair to say that in my first ambassadorial assignment, to which I had come under President Truman after retiring from business, I was an amateur in diplomacy. I conclude from subsequent events that I was judged to have performed with greater aptitude in my next ambassadorial assignment; and I hope with still greater aptitude—gained from experience on the job—in the next following ones. What emerges from my own experience and that of others is the need for on-the-job training. Because this can be a costly process, the question, then, is how to identify the best qualified people for ambassadorships.

That is what this modest study is supposed to deal with. In line with the Institute's chosen emphasis on operational rather than policy aspects of diplomacy, we try to examine what are the requirements of the job; we look into qualifications needed to enable a person to meet those requirements; and we address the prickly but important subject of where the best ambassadors come from—in other words, how one can find the future ones who will provide the best services in protecting and advancing a country's interests and the peace of the world.

1

Summary of the Problem

How relevant is an ambassador in today's "modern diplomacy"? What are his traditional and new functions? Where does one find the best people to appoint as ambassadors? Nowhere are these questions better laid out than in a study issued by the Senate Foreign Relations Committee in 1981 entitled *The Ambassador in U.S. Foreign Policy: Changing Patterns in Roles, Selection, and Designations*. The Chairman, Charles H. Percy of Illinois, notes in his introduction that the study, prepared by the Congressional Research Service of the Library of Congress, "is intended to provide an overview of the role of the ambassador in American diplomatic tradition and practice, and to identify areas of controversy which most frequently arise in contemporary discussion of the appropriate role of the ambassador in the conduct of U.S. foreign policy."

We feature here selections from "The Changing Role of the Chief of Mission," "Career vs. Non-Career" and a relevant portion of "Findings." Not reproduced is a large part of the study that deals with an interesting new issue, the growing use of the title of ambassador for persons who are entrusted with certain negotiations or who represent the U.S. in international organizations or as roving ambassadors or ambassadors-at-large, who do not head diplomatic missions. (The study refers to such positions when it speaks of a "proliferation" of ambassadorial appointments.)

With regard to the multifarious problems of coordination between the various elements of diplomatic missions, the Senate report notes that while this presents problems it is not really an issue. In contrast to the different points of view about functions and selection, it says: "There is one area of unanimity—if not within the whole government, at least in Congress, the White House, and the Foreign Service— that within a foreign country the ambassador must be the paramount authority for coordination and administration of American foreign policy."

The Ambassador in U.S. Foreign Policy

THE CHANGING ROLE OF THE CHIEF OF MISSION

While chiefs of mission heading U.S. Embassies abroad are not the only type of ambassadorial appointees, they are by far the most numerous, and are also the focal point for much of the current debate over the alleged decline of the ambassador's role in the conduct of American foreign policy. Although there is no single criterion dividing the numerous commentators on the subject, there are two discernible schools of thought on the current state of the American chief of mission.

One view holds that circumstances have relegated ambassadors to the role of managers of embassies with no substantive impact on foreign policy.[1] This position is usually taken by those who assert that a "new diplomacy" has emerged in the aftermath of World War II replacing the traditional bilateral "tête-à-tête" diplomatic intercourse of the 19th century. Their argument is that modern communications, the growth of bureaucracy, the advent of multilateral (and increasingly technical) international relationships have made the ambassador an anachronism. The focus of decision making has moved away from the ambassador and the Department of State and into the White House and Washington's national security apparatus where virtually all important decisions are now made.

If lengthy negotiations are expected, a team of experts is dispatched from Washington. If a crisis develops, a special team of presidential advisors is assembled in the White House situation room. If informed analysis and information are required, the Central Intelligence Agency (CIA) or the National Security Agency (NSA) are consulted. In short, the ambassador no longer plays a meaningful role in developing or even managing American foreign policy. Rather, he is seen as merely a tool for its implementation, and is

From *The Ambassador in U.S. Foreign Policy: Changing Patterns in Roles, Selection, and Designations,* prepared for the Committee on Foreign Relations, United States Senate, by the Foreign Affairs and National Defense Division, Congressional Research Service, Library of Congress (Washington: U.S. Government Printing Office, 1981), pp. 2–7, 15–16.

[1]See for example, J. Robert Schaetzel, Modernizing the Role of the Ambassador in Elmer Plischke, *Modern Diplomacy,* pp. 262–276. Also, Stanley Karnow, Today's Diplomatic Modes Diminish Foreign Service, *Washington Star,* January 6, 1980: C3.

told via satellite (encoded cable) what is expected of him. The rationale given in 1980 by career Foreign Service Officer and American Consul in Moscow, Thomas Hutson, to explain his resignation provides the most recent example supporting this perspective. Hutson declared, "We don't need an ambassador in Moscow . . . because he has nothing to do."[2] An even more succinct statement of this position is the quote attributed to former Secretary of State Henry Kissinger: "Ambassadors don't count anymore."[3]

The opposing point of view is most often advanced by career Foreign Service Officers (FSOs).[4] They maintain that while modern communications have allowed ambassadors to be more directly responsive to Washington, this by no means obviates the need for high-level personal contact in foreign countries. In diplomacy, they point out, it is not only what is said that counts but also how it is said and explained. Furthermore, of the traditional four functions of the ambassador—negotiating, reporting, representation and consular duties—only the responsibility for a select class of negotiations (those highly technical in nature or of such magnitude that they demand the presence of heads of state) has diminished. In all other areas the responsibilities of the ambassador have grown with the increasing complexity of the international system. Without U.S. Ambassadors stationed abroad, Washington would soon be inundated with minor policy questions and American interests abroad would eventually suffer. In sum, they argue, it is necessary to have an experienced and knowledgeable representative in residence abroad to orchestrate U.S. programs in that country and insure tactful and accurate articulation of American positions on the myriad issues confronting the international community. The hostage crisis in Iran offers, according to this viewpoint, a current example of how difficult negotiations can be without high-level personal contact. A bad situation became an impossible one without a U.S. representative on the scene to utilize domestic sources of information, to monitor and evaluate changing conditions, and to provide a reliable

---

[2]Don Oberdorfer, Consular Officer Quits in Protest Over U.S. Policy, *Washington Post*, April 12, 1980: A1, A13.

[3]Don Cook, For Diplomatic Service, More Diplomacy, *Los Angeles Times*, February 15, 1977: PT 2, 2, 5.

[4]See for example, Foy D. Kohler, Role of the Ambassador: Existing Status and Proposal for Improvement; and Charles W. Thayer, Case for Professional Diplomats, both in Plischke, *Modern Diplomacy*. Also, Why Not Send the Best as Ambassadors? *New York Times*, December 18, 1976:23.

conduit for communication flow. With no Iranian representatives in Washington capable of speaking authoritatively for Iran, and U.S. representatives held incommunicado, the United States ultimately had to turn to the Algerian Government as an intermediary in order to find a solution. "Long distance diplomacy" via the international media is simply not effective as it is invariably marred by rhetoric and posturing.

In contrast to the discord created by these different points of view, there is one area of unanimity—if not within the whole government, at least in Congress, the White House, and the Foreign Service—that within a foreign country the ambassador must be the paramount authority for coordination and administration of American policy. The management of multiplying U.S. programs abroad has been a major problem for ambassadors over the last several decades. The origins of the problem can be traced to 1927 when then Secretary of Commerce Herbert Hoover convinced Congress that the Department of Commerce needed its own representatives overseas.[5] Since then, many more Government agencies have made the same argument successfully, the latest being the Department of Energy. In 1971 less than 15 percent of all U.S. Government personnel stationed abroad were State Department employees, and as of September 29, 1980, the figure was still only 23 percent.[6] Managing personnel who feel more responsible to their respective agencies back in the United States than to the ambassador in the field is difficult. In recognition of the problem every President since Harry Truman has moved to consolidate the authority of the ambassador, usually via personal directives.[7] Congress has acted similarly.

In the State Department/USIA Authorization Act of 1975 Congress mandated full responsibility to the ambassador for the "direction, coordination, and supervision of all U.S. Government officials and employees in that country except for personnel under the command of a U.S. area military commander" (Sec. 12, P.L. 93-475). The Act also prescribes coordination between U.S. agencies with overseas personnel and the chief of mission, and holds these agen-

[5]W. Wendell Blancké, *The Foreign Service of the United States*, New York, Praeger, 1969, p. 21.

[6]*U.S. News and World Report*, September 29, 1980: p. 36.

[7]U.S. Library of Congress, Congressional Research Service, History and Effect of President Kennedy's 1961 Memorandum to U.S. Ambassadors, Report by Allan S. Nanes, Washington, January 30, 1973, pp. 3–10, 12–17. Also, Carter Tells Embassies, *Federal Times*, December 5, 1977:20.

cies responsible for insuring their personnel comply with the directives of the chief of mission. The same provisions were incorporated in the Foreign Service Act of 1980 (Sec. 207, P.L. 96-465).

CAREER VERSUS NON-CAREER

Intertwined with the debate over the evolution of the Ambassador's role and importance is the perennial issue of career versus non-career ambassadors. Under President Truman almost one-half of all ambassadors were career FSOs. By the time President Eisenhower left office the percentage had risen to about 75 percent career. According to Elmer Plischke, the percentage of career ambassadors fluctuated between 65 and 75 percent during the interval between the Eisenhower and Ford administrations.[8] It has remained in the 70th percentile range since the beginning of the Ford administration. Despite the rise in the percentage of career ambassadors, the issue has not died. The American Foreign Service Association, the professional organization and labor union for Foreign Service Officers, recommends that 90 percent of U.S. Ambassadors be career diplomats.[9] And even though FSOs applaud the increase in career ambassadors, they are quick to point out that political appointees still occupy most of the important posts.[10]

Nevertheless, support for the alternative extreme—a majority of political appointees—is seldom expressed. Almost all concerned seem to agree that flagrant use of ambassadorial nominations by the President to meet patronage needs is wrong when the result is an obviously incompetent candidate. Likewise, most observers agree that a well-qualified non-career ambassador can be highly effective. The disagreement arises as one moves to the middle ground and considers whether or not the President should use political appointees as a means of enhancing his control over the administration of U.S. foreign policy, even if it means the loss of some institutional expertise.

Those who favor the appointment of non-career ambassadors contend that Foreign Service officers have been bureaucratized, made overly timid, bogged down in inefficiency and locked into

---

[8]Plischke, *United States Diplomats and their Missions*, pp. 104–5.

[9]Bill Andronicos, AFSA Calls for Care in Naming Diplomats, *Federal Times*, January 3, 1977:7.

[10]Schaetzel, Modernizing the Role of the Ambassador in Plischke, *Modern Diplomacy*, p. 267.

bilateralist views of U.S. foreign policy interests ("localitis") which inhibits their perception of broader foreign policy goals. According to this argument, most FSOs are better at representing the interests of the states to which they are accredited than those of the United States. In developing their contacts in a foreign country, absorbing the local culture, and digesting their host nation's point of view they lose sight of U.S. interests, and when reminded of this, still avoid pressing the U.S. position lest they alienate their hosts. Further, FSOs make the mistake of assuming that cordial relations are good relations. What America needs, these critics argue, are ambassadors who are loyal to the President and willing to vigorously pursue his foreign policy.[11]

The opposing view holds that political appointees are transient amateurs and an unnecessary intrusion. It is not a question of whether the President will have his "own men" in American Embassies, because FSOs are by law the President's men. Adherents of this perspective do not recognize the need for non-career ambassadors on the grounds of loyalty. Former FSO and Ambassador Charles W. Yost was categorical on this point: "In my thirty-five years in the Foreign Service I never encountered an officer who was disloyal or disobedient to an incumbent president."[12] As for the argument that FSOs tend to side with their host states on issues, State Department personnel are rotated from country to country frequently to help avoid this problem, even though the practice tends to undermine area expertise. In addition, there is no assurance that a non-career ambassador will agree with presidential policy and his lack of "professional mores" may make him more prone to act on his own opinions. Finally, as former FSO and Ambassador Martin Herz testified before Congress, demands for what one Secretary of State had called "positive loyalty" evoke memories of McCarthyism.[13] There is a need for different opinions on the conduct of U.S. American foreign policy. The long break in U.S.-Chinese relations might have been less severe and the conflict in Vietnam less protracted, they contend, had there been a greater willingness to listen to the opinions of career FSOs.

---

[11]See John Krizay, Clientitus, Corpulence, and Clones at State—the Symptomatology of a Sick Department, *Policy Review*, No. 4, Spring 1978: 39–55.

[12]Charles W. Yost, Still Too Many Amateur Ambassadors, *Christian Science Monitor*, November 10, 1977:27.

[13]U.S. Congress, Senate, Committee on Foreign Relations, Foreign Service Act of 1979,

Congress has not remained aloof from the career versus non-career issue. Some have argued that representation costs in the major foreign capitals are prohibitive for any but the independently wealthy, and in the past many non-career ambassadors have also been large political campaign contributors. But in 1973 Congress added a provision to the Department of State Authorization Act (Sec. 6, P.L. 93-126) requiring each ambassadorial candidate to disclose to the Senate Foreign Relations Committee chairman any campaign contributions. The following year, Congress stipulated that statements of these contributions be published in the Congressional

---

"Those who favor the appointment of non-career ambassadors contend that Foreign Service officers have been bureaucratized, made overly timid, bogged down in inefficiency and locked into bilateralist views of U.S. foreign policy interests ("localitis") which inhibits their perception of broader foreign policy goals. . . . The opposing view holds that political appointees are transient amateurs and an unnecessary intrusion."

Record. Along with the $1,000 personal campaign contribution ceiling this has helped curtail the practice of rewarding otherwise unqualified wealthy contributors with ambassadorial appointments.

The same provisions were included in the Foreign Service Act of 1980. The Act is also explicit on campaign contributions: they "should not be a factor in the appointment of an individual as a chief of mission" (Sec. 304, P.L. 96-465). In 1974 the Senate initially accepted a provision within the Foreign Assistance Act of 1974 which would have required that not less than 80 percent of all ambassadorial posts be held by the career Foreign Service officers. However, this measure was dropped when the bill was recommitted to committee. Senator Charles Mathias, who sponsored the provision, tried again in 1976 with a 75 percent FSO requirement but a conference committee removed the Mathias language and instead simply expressed the non-binding sense of the Congress that "a greater number of

---

Hearings on S. 1450, 96th Congress, 1st session. July 27, December 14, 19, 1979 (Washington, U.S. Government Printing Office, 1980), pp. 215–220.

positions of ambassador should be occupied by career personnel in the Foreign Service." (Sec. 120, P.L. 94-350, 90 Stat. 829). However, the Foreign Service Act of 1980 does place a ceiling of 5 percent on the number of non-career members that can be named to [the] new Senior Foreign Service created by the Act. This provision is seen within the Foreign Service as a helpful protection against any future attempts to "politicize" the top echelon of the Service.[14]

With respect to qualifications, the Committee on Foreign Relations has become progressively more stringent in its demands that ambassadorial candidates exhibit competence relevant to their intended assignment, especially foreign language capabilities. This intention was specifically included in the Foreign Service Act of 1980 which stated that ambassadors should possess:

> . . . clearly demonstrated competence to perform the duties of a chief of mission, including, to the maximum extent practicable, a useful knowledge of the principal language or dialect of the country in which the individual is to serve, and knowledge and understanding of the history, the culture, the economic and political institutions, and the interests of that country and its people. [Considering this], positions as chief of mission should normally be accorded to career members of the Service, though circumstances will warrant appointments from time to time of qualified individuals who are not career members of the Service.[15]

In addition, the Act also contains a clause sponsored by Senator Claiborne Pell requiring the President to submit to the Committee on Foreign Relations a report on the "demonstrated competence" of each of his nominations.[16] President Carter, who signed the bill into law also issued Executive Order 11970 in 1977 which created a President's Advisory Board on Ambassadorial Appointments. The declared purpose of the Board was to screen out all unqualified candidates, but there have been mixed opinions as to the success of the endeavor.

---

[14]Information received in telephone conversation with Bill Bacchus, Director, Office of Program Coordination, Bureau of Personnel, Department of State, December 1980. See also, Kenneth W. Bleakley, A Plus for Career Diplomacy, *Washington Post*, November 21, 1980: A16.

[15]U.S. Congress, Committee on Conference, Foreign Service Act of 1980, Conference Report to accompany H.R. 6790, House Report No. 96-1432, 96th Congress, 2d session (Washington, U.S. Government Printing Office, 1980), A16. [Editor's Note: The full text of this section of the Act and a related section are included in Chapter 9, pp. 180–82 below.]

[16]Ibid.

FINDINGS

. . . Whether or not ambassadors will be able to contribute to a successful foreign policy also depends on administration attitudes. Ambassadors can be ignored or utilized. As noted by many informed observers and two of the most extensive government studies on the State Department (the Macomber Report, *Diplomacy for the 70's,* and the "Murphy Commission's" 1975 Report),[17] every President since Truman, whether initially well disposed toward the State Department or not, has quickly developed a mistrust for that agency. For whatever reason, Presidents have concluded that the State Department (and by extension ambassadors and the Foreign Service) is not responsive to their policy directives. This has led to the use of alternative means of diplomacy, which, while sometimes useful, tend to contribute to confusion in the long run. Because, in the final analysis, the Department of State is the most logical tool for implementing foreign policy, it appears counterproductive to ignore it. Consequently, it is important that the President's confidence in his own diplomatic corps be restored.

Among other things, this means that while ambassadors need to feel free to vigorously communicate their points of view back to those in Washington responsible for policy formation, they must be willing to "hew the line" once policy is made. Toward this end it would seem advisable for incoming administrations to discuss principal policy goals with prospective ambassadorial candidates before nominating them in order to clarify their willingness to support policy once it has been articulated.

The President's attitude toward his diplomatic representatives is also determined by their qualifications. It is doubtful whether any ambassador can serve the President or his country well if the requisite knowledge for understanding U.S. policy and the skills for implementing it are lacking. It bears pointing out that the issue here is qualifications and not the career or non-career status of the candidate. Both types of appointees have served the United States well. A flexible and eclectic approach would seem to be implied.

---

[17]U.S. Department of State, *Diplomacy for the 70's* (Washington, U.S. Government Printing Office, 1970), p. 305; U.S. Commission on the Organization of the Government for the Conduct of Foreign Policy: Report (Washington, The Commission: U.S. Government Printing Office, 1975), p. 108; and also see Laurence Silberman, Toward Presidential Control of the State Department, *Foreign Affairs,* Vol. 57. Spring 1979: 872–893 [included in Chapter 6, pp. 119–27 below—Ed.].

For example, in addition to the individual candidate, the country of assignment needs to be considered. Some countries, such as Great Britain (which has never had a career ambassador from America) and the Soviet Union (which distrusts career ambssadors, considering them "hidebound"), seem amenable to non-career appointments. Other nations, such as Canada and Luxembourg, have taken affront at non-career ambassadors and strongly requested career appointments. Such idiosyncrasies are usefully considered in conjunction with the ambassadorial candidates' personal qualifications. But more importantly, the selection of ambassadors should not be viewed as primarily an occasion for paying off political debts or acknowledging years of dedicated government service. The non-career candidates who are selected for domestic political reasons and later fail to support or pursue effectively the President's policy may also be difficult to remove from their posts for domestic political reasons. Career candidates who are selected pro forma for their past record may not be amenable to the President's policy and style preferences. Consequently the candidates' qualifications and willingness to diligently implement the administration's policy remain as central criteria of selection.

Finally, it should be said that all of these observations are of little value, if, as some have suggested, the ambassador is an anachronism in a world of instant global communications and centralized decision-making apparatus. Technocratic societies emphasize problem solving by organization, procedure, and with topical experts. These factors, and the preference for measuring performance quantitatively, tend to obscure the intangible but often invaluable contributions of human assets. As some venerable practitioners of the diplomatic service have quietly observed on occasion, the best insurance for a dynamic and effective foreign policy is the placement of highly qualified personnel in key positions. In the complex international arena of conflict and cooperation, this would seem to be especially true for American Ambassadors.

2

Is the Role Obsolete?

The advent of rapid means of travel and telecommunication has clearly brought changes to the conduct of diplomacy. How significant are the changes? Is traditional diplomacy obsolete?

Some believe that ambassadors have now been demoted to glorified messengers when they are not bypassed altogether by direct government-to-government communication. Certainly the new ease of travel has meant that ambassadors have more and more high-level visitors to accommodate, leading some of them to complain that they are becoming glorified innkeepers. On the other hand, modern technology has also added to the substantive work of embassies and ambassadors. This chapter focuses on the changing requirements of the profession and the relevance of ambassadors in today's diplomacy.

The article by **Barbara Gamarekian,** a Washington correspondent of the *New York Times,* is an example of the way basic questions and issues about ambassadorial appointments are treated in the news pages. The three remaining items are by diplomatic practitioners. **Berndt von Staden,** whose essay deals with the changing patterns and new responsibilities, was for six years ambassador of the German Federal Republic in Washington and is presently State Secretary [deputy foreign minister] in Bonn. **John G. H. Halstead,** who was Canada's ambassador to the German Federal Republic and to NATO, is currently an Associate of the Institute for the Study of Diplomacy. **Kingman Brewster** was president of Yale University before becoming American ambassador to the Court of St. James. He is at present partner in a law firm in New York.

We thank the *New York Times* and Ambassador Brewster for permission to reprint the first and last items, respectively, of this chapter.

Has Diplomacy Become Out of Date?

Barbara Gamarekian

In this era of computers, satellite communication and secure telephone lines, is old-fashioned diplomacy out of date? Have striped-pants diplomacy and the diplomatic social whirl been supplanted by the new technology?

Yes, says Zbigniew Brzezinksi, a former national security adviser. "It's a boondoggle, a waste of money," he said of traditional diplomacy.

No, says Count Wilhelm Wachtmeister, the Swedish Ambassador to the United States. "I take issue with the suggestion that daily diplomacy has lost importance," he said. "Technically, it is simpler, we can send a telefax home. But the very ease of communication has meant broadened contacts and has made the daily diplomatic life and tasks more important. A diplomat has much more to do. Heads of state can't talk about all the nuts and bolts of daily diplomatic give and take."

And so goes the debate.

Charles William Maynes, a former State Department official and currently editor of the magazine *Foreign Policy*, said that advances in communication had "strengthened the role of a good ambassador and weakened the role of a bad ambassador."

"It is true that the British Foreign Minister can pick up the telephone and call Ronald Reagan, and a *New York Times* reporter can get a story on the President's desk as fast as the Ambassador in Moscow can," Mr. Maynes said. "And that undermines the authority of an ambassador because he no longer has a monopoly on communication.

"But on the other hand, faster communications have also made it possible for a good ambassador to be a direct participant in policy decisions. If he is considered strong and able, secure communications open up the possibility for an ambassador to be a part of the working process."

Winston Lord, president of the Council on Foreign Relations, points out that ambassadors are in the position of being able to report on the internal machinations of a capital city. "You can deploy special envoys to the Falklands or the Middle East," he said, "but it is only the local ambassador who can report on what is really going on."

"Secondly," said Mr. Lord, "it is important for an ambassador to represent his country. That can mean everything from getting out and around the country and promoting a good public image to lobbying Congress and the executive branch."

But Mr. Brzezinski remains adamant.

"Governments should conduct business the way international corporations do," he said, "with special representatives in modest offices utilizing telecommunications. The whole diplomatic system needs to be modernized so that it can operate with more rapidity instead of maintaining the extraordinary costly establishments and entertainments.

"For the most part serious business is not conducted by the ambassador. In my time there were about a dozen ambassadors with whom I had worthwhile exchanges and learned a good deal. But usually it is just an exhausting exercise and a waste of time."

William H. Gleysteen, director of the Washington office of the Asia Society and a former career Foreign Service officer, has worked both sides of the ambassadorial street. He served in many diplomatic posts including that of United States Ambassador to Korea from 1978 to 1981, a time of uprisings, a Presidential assassination and an army coup. In Washington, he has worked for people like former Secretary of State Henry A. Kissinger, "who believes," he said, "that ambassadors are nothing more than lackeys anyway."

"Compared to 19th-century diplomacy where you would have ministers in China and Japan who were on a very long tether and could only operate through letters coming by sea," said Mr. Gleysteen, "there is no doubt that the new procedures have limited the role of an envoy to being largely an agent rather than an independent actor. It is one more significant factor eroding the independence or autonomy of our missions abroad, but it need not undermine an effective operation."

"Even with the new technology," he added, "even under someone like Henry Kissinger who was almost contemptuous of ambassadors—and as a result I was under pressure to limit their scope for action—even under those conditions, I thought some of them did a pretty good job of standing their ground."

But for the diplomat, there is another communications problem that is ageless and unrelated to the new technology: How to get attention.

"Getting attention is a terrible problem for ambassadors," said Mr. Gleysteen. "A good ambassador must know how to write, whom to write, who is handling the telephone at the other end, what the Washington landscape is. The fanciest communications are meaningless if the person on the other end of the line has no influence, or if the telegram is so long or boring that the President will never see it."

Changing Patterns and New Responsibilities

Berndt von Staden

The tasks of an ambassador can probably not be described in terms that have universal validity. The ambassador of a western industrial country, for example, has highly varied tasks depending on whether he is accredited to a country similar to his own or to a developing country and whether relations with the country to which he is accredited are friendly or of a more or less antagonistic nature. The following observations, which express the author's personal views, are based exclusively on the experience gained during six years as ambassador in Washington. Some of the judgments based on this experience may have general validity, but many surely do not. This contribution is therefore but a stone in a mosaic, albeit a stone without which the overall picture might be incomplete.

Political intercourse between allied and friendly countries, especially in the western world but certainly not only there, takes place today mainly on a multilateral basis or bilaterally through direct contacts between governments, whether through the increased use of "visiting diplomacy," through cabled messages, or—not least—through telephone calls. This applies not only to the political level of heads of state and government as well as foreign and other ministers but also to the working level. Professional diplomacy is, therefore, deprived of many of its traditional functions, but there is no point in lamenting this development. It would be just as futile as yearning for the days of mail coaches. In this unstable, increasingly interdependent and shrinking world it would be irresponsible if those engaged in the international domain did not avail themselves of every opportunity afforded by modern means of communication and transport. This trend is undoubtedly far from having run its course. As communications technology is being constantly improved, more and more new opportunities will arise for direct contacts between governments and administrations.

Consequently, it comes as no surprise that doubts are voiced as to whether traditional diplomacy still has a useful function to perform. This is a good question, but it is essentially posed in the wrong way. For what is "traditional diplomacy"? Of course, some tasks disappear or diminish in importance, while others gain in significance or new ones emerge. It is therefore only natural that in this changing world the functions and working methods of diplomats should change as well. Only the diplomat who does not realize or accept this runs the risk of calling his own usefulness into question.

Modern means of communication and transport not only facilitate direct contacts between governments and those active in the political sphere. They also enlarge the areas of contact between countries and increase their interdependence. At the same time, the number of people involved in the political process is constantly rising—in the political and parliamentary fields, in the media, in the relevant social groups, and finally among the representatives of public opinion in general. But this growing interdependence and enlarged number of participants is not necessarily accompanied by more intensified mutual knowledge and understanding or a greater willingness to get to know one another. The homogeneous group of people who in the nineteenth century, for instance, controlled the fortunes of Europe—by and large with some degree of success—no longer exists. On the contrary, it is noticeable that some of today's leadership elements are even becoming more inward-looking in their attitudes.

What conclusions can we draw from this for the tasks of a present-day ambassador? To start with the simplest one: As a result of the intensification of visits, the ambassador is increasingly becoming the head of a "service enterprise" responsible for preparing and carrying out smoothly, effectively and properly this form of direct intercourse between his government and that of the host country. This task should not be underrated. Although, on the face of it, it is an organizational one, it requires political acumen and good contacts. In the field of actual substantive tasks, most of the negotiating functions that once devolved upon ambassadors have disappeared. But at the same time the tasks of presentation and interpretation have grown to an equal or even larger extent. In our democratic age of the media, the ambassador must in this respect meet greater requirements than ever before; he must constantly endeavor to present, substantiate and canvass support for the interests and policies of his country. He must do so not only vis-à-vis public opinion in the host country, especially its media, but also vis-à-vis the circles of direct political relevance, and last but not least the government itself. To express this in commercial terms: The ambassador is today less involved in production than in marketing. There are evidently no limits at all to this task since it is hardly likely that the market for information and interpretation in our mass society could ever become saturated.

This task must, incidentally, be performed in both directions. The ambassador must also keep his own government informed of the situation, developments and prospective events in the host country so that it can effectively attend to its interests in good time. Even by exploiting all modern means of communication, much of this information cannot be obtained from sporadic contacts, by visits, letter or telephone. To obtain this what is necessary is constant observation, great familiarity with the terrain, and the cultivation of the right personal contacts on a broad scale.

This twofold task of interpretation and information naturally includes the exercise of some influence as well. This occurs more or less automatically in the process of collecting and evaluating and interpreting information, and is indeed desirable. Finally, the ambassador continues to be the man on the spot who must always be at the disposal of the host country's representatives for talks, consultation and the settlement of differences. He can be asked for information, requested to forward messages for which other channels are unsuitable, and his advice can be sought if one wants to make sure that one is taking the right course and action. This function is of course not only a passive but also an active one. The ambassador must himself take the initiative if he has the impression that an opportunity is being missed, a danger overlooked or an error committed. To a certain extent, the remarks that Edward VII is said to have made about the role of the British king apply: He must know everything, he must encourage and warn.

The role of the "man on the spot" also has two aspects. The main precept of the ambassador's activities is, admittedly, fidelity to the policies and interests of his own country. But he can, in the final analysis, only serve these policies and interests effectively if he at the same time solicits and obtains the trust of the host country, in other words, if he is also "loyal" to the host country in a manner commensurate with their mutual interests. An ambassador is certainly not impartial, but he is nonetheless to a certain extent an honest broker.

The demands that successful performance of the tasks described above places on the personality and qualifications of an ambassador should not be underestimated. This attempted job description shows that ideally he must combine highly contrasting characteristics. He must be able to act with authority at all levels, but must at all times be willing to subordinate his own image and identity to the matter in question. He must be independent, yet exercise a high degree of discipline. In order to obtain trust and respect he must always comport himself as a man of principles and convictions, but he must never forget that he represents government policy and cannot, therefore, assert views that are only his own personal way of looking at things.

Since trust is the most precious asset in international relations in this precarious world, the ambassador must do his utmost to solicit, obtain and nurture trust. At the same time, however, he must act in such a way that he does not detract from the interests of his country, be they substantive or tactical in nature. He must be a salesman, yet discreet; a man of action, yet not overweening; always alert, yet calm; willing to take risks if necessary, yet circumspect. He needs a sound knowledge of the subject matter in order to be able to interpret it and discuss it with others, and must be tactful as well as experienced in dealing with other people. He must be conversant with the environment in which he performs his functions and must be well-educated, including in history, yet must not become an academic but remain a practical man.

Do such fabulously adept creatures really exist? If so, where can they be found? Well, one probably comes across them everywhere, but only very rarely. One can, as a rule, only get near to an ideal but never reach it. However, it should never be forgotten that the ambassador has an important and difficult job that places great demands on his capacities and expertise. Like good physicians or good bankers, good ambassadors do not fall from heaven. Rather, they mature gradually through their education, training and experience until they ultimately resemble the wondrous creature described above.

Today's Ambassador

John G. H. Halstead

As long as the international community is composed of independent sovereign states engaged in a perpetual struggle with one another, diplomacy is bound to be a tool, like military might, for the enhancement of each state's power and the pursuit of its national interests. At the same time, technological and sociological changes have been altering both the framework and the methods of international relations, making them far more complex than ever before, bringing home the implications of interdependence for this "global village" we live in and raising the spectre of global annihilation. Even for superpowers, diplomacy today must involve the acceptance of constraints on their pursuit of purely national ends. For smaller and middle powers, there is no choice but to seek to reconcile divergent national interests and to settle conflicts peacefully.

The present day organization of international relations reflects these changing conditions. Bilateral relations have been influenced by the growing involvement of government not only in the everyday life of the nation but also in the increasingly intricate web of international exchanges. Multilateral relations have been shaped by the growing number of intergovernmental bodies set up to resolve disputes and to promote cooperation. As the international environment has evolved, so have the functions of diplomacy and the role of the ambassador, aided by the enormous progress in communications and the information revolution. While his authority and prestige may, in some respects, have declined, his field of action and the scope of his operations have in many ways expanded and opened new opportunities for him.

Today, instant communications have transformed all diplomatic posts into branch offices of headquarters and heads of post into branch managers. There is practically no detail of a post's operations too small to escape detailed instructions from headquarters, even in areas where the crucial element is the local situation and the ambassador should be in the best position to know that situation. Foreign ministries and members of government are in direct touch with one another, and jet travel has ushered in the era of visit diplomacy and wall-to-wall international meetings. These activities are of course to be welcomed to the extent they intensify international cooperation, but there is no doubt they make the ambassador's task more difficult.

The information revolution has produced more media participation in international affairs, more public demand for information and more distrust of diplomatic secrecy. It has given the public the impression of being in instant touch with events around the world and has even produced the view that diplomats may be obsolete. If TV, radio and the press can bring us all the information we need, would it not be more effective, and cheaper, to send members of the government or experts abroad when something has to be negotiated with foreign governments? What this leaves out of account is the essential role of diplomats in preparing the ground for negotiations on the basis of mutual knowledge and confidence, in correcting inaccurate or misleading media reports and in nurturing the delicate process of mutual accommodation and compromise away from the glare of publicity.

There has, in fact, been a steady expansion of the ambassador's functions, both quantitatively and qualitatively. Today he is involved, beyond classical diplomatic exchanges between governments, in economic and commercial diplomacy, in cultural diplomacy, and in public diplomacy of all kinds. He is dealing not only with other diplomats and officials but with a broad cross section of the public, such as businessmen, artists, students, and the press. And a growing proportion of his staff is made up of specialists in various fields— commerce, culture, immigration—not traditionally part of the diplomatic establishment.

The ambassador acts as a kind of hyphen not just between his own government and the government to which he is accredited but more broadly between the two nations. The image he projects of his country and his people, of his government's interests and intentions, can have an important effect on the media and on influential circles in his host country and can color the context in which their decisions are made. It can suggest ideas of stability and consistency or it can do the opposite. And when he represents a country with a federal system, such as Canada, he must be sure to speak and act for *all* constituent parts of the federation. In the reverse direction he has to understand what makes the host country tick, how to analyze its purposes accurately and how to assess its main trends.

He should be able to evaluate its interests but should be careful not to promote them. He should explain its policies but not excuse them.

It is important for the ambassador to build up a network of contacts not only in governmental circles but also in the private sector. For this purpose personal relations of mutual respect are essential and social activities have their part to play. In the past there has been public criticism in some countries of extravagance in this connection but it is my experience that the judicious use of entertaining can be very effective, provided it is selective and well focused. It is also my experience that the ambassador's wife, too often taken for granted or neglected by foreign offices and the public

---

"There has, in fact, been a steady expansion of the ambassador's functions, both quantitatively and qualitatively. Today he is involved, beyond classical diplomatic exchanges between governments, in economic and commercial diplomacy, in cultural diplomacy, and in public diplomacy of all kinds. He is dealing not only with other diplomats and officials but with a broad cross section of the public, such as businessmen, artists, students, and the press."

---

alike, can actually play a more significant role today than in the past. She can make her own contribution to projecting her country's image not only through entertaining but also by pursuing her personal or professional interests in the host country.

Representing Canada in the Federal Republic of Germany, I found these to be both challenging and rewarding functions. They involved me in developing exchanges of mutual benefit across the whole gamut of the relationship and in seeking to reconcile differences of view and conflicting interests where necessary. In the private sector, I saw my function as opening up communications and putting people with convergent interests in touch with one another. Sometimes I was able to see concrete and satisfying results from my labors, as when a society for Canadian studies was formed by German academics with my help. Occasionally I had to recognize that there are conflicts of interest that cannot be bridged, and then the ambassador has to be clear where he stands. Such a time arrived in Bonn when the divergence between Canadian and German policies on nuclear proliferation came to a head over the sale of a nuclear reactor to Argentina.

The methods of operation at multilateral posts are significantly different, as I found when I was Deputy Permanent Representative to the United Nations in New York in the 1950s and more recently, Ambassador to NATO in Brussels. There my dealings were almost exclusively with other diplomats, though of many nations, and the subject matter was more highly specialized. The challenge was to develop skills of negotiation and a grasp of technical material which went far beyond what would normally be required in bilateral posts. Although intellectually stimulating, it could also be frustrating because of the enormous disproportion between words and deeds, between good intentions and concrete achievements.

Have the qualities needed by a good ambassador changed along with his changing role in the new diplomacy? I believe they have in fact remained remarkably constant, and I group them in three broad categories. First are the qualities required to deal effectively with people, to create credibility rather than distrust, to foster cooperation rather than confrontation and to put one's self in other people's shoes. For this he must have a combination of integrity and adaptability, consistency and tolerance and sound judgment of character. He must judge who are the best contacts and when to go to them. In Bonn, for example, I was fortunate in having access to Chancellor Schmidt when necessary but I used it exceedingly sparingly, preferring to maintain close touch with his immediate aides and with a select number of state secretaries for normal business.

Second are the abilities needed to deal successfully with dynamic situations. For this an ambassador must be able to think clearly and ask the right questions (i.e., to analyse) and to take timely action (i.e., to decide on the least unsatisfactory course in a situation where like as not the choice is not between a good solution and a bad one but between a number of undesirable alternatives). Third is a capacity to communicate ideas precisely and concisely, to marshall arguments coherently and persuasively and to negotiate effectively.

To these I would add another requirement whose importance has, I think, been underestimated in the past, in Canada at least: that is a working knowledge of the language of the host country. English- and French-speaking diplomats undoubtedly have an advantage abroad because there are few places where English, and to a lesser extent French, are not understood, but it is an advantage that is too often abused. There is no substitute for approaching a man in his own language as a way of establishing a relationship of mutual sympathy and respect. And there is no substitute for language as a vehicle for understanding a nation's character and culture.

In some foreign services there has in recent time been a great emphasis on management and on management theories and techniques. I think it is true that in the past the tradition for diplomatic officers has been to concentrate on political analysis and diplomatic skills and to leave management to administrators. There is a need for modern management skills but they need to be put in proper perspective. Techniques for organizing, directing, and controlling resources are important but they are means, not ends, and they are meaningful in the diplomatic context only to the extent they serve the ends of formulating and implementing foreign policy.

In the last analysis, a country's diplomacy depends on the quality of the human resources it can deploy in support of its interests, and an ambassador is front and center in that context.

Advice to a New Ambassador

Kingman Brewster

One of the most disconcerting things awaiting a new ambassador nowadays is the somewhat insulting journalistic query, "Do you think ambassadors matter anymore? You know, now that anyone can pick up the phone and talk directly with his counterpart or be there in a flash if a personal tête-à-tête is called for?"

Your answer will be an irritated, "Yes, of course I matter"—all the while muttering to yourself about whoever the current counterpart of Zbig Brzezinski may be, who acts as though you didn't exist (perhaps because he wishes you didn't).

There will be times when you will sit like a student waiting for his grades. This is when you have sent reams of cables saying what Lord Carrington intends to take up with the Secretary of State, what his positions will be, what his exasperation points are. When the two secretaries finally do meet, there you will sit like a deaf-mute as the conversation between them proceeds, wondering whether you had sized everything up right. Very nervous business. But it should be. For by far the most important ambassadorial function is still to prevent the "host" government from being taken by surprise by anything we do; and, more important, to protect our government from being caught off guard by anything "they" think or say or do.

Embassies are crucial to this function. If your staff is as good as mine was, you ought to have a better feel for the local situation, the local feelings, the local intentions and the local responses than even the most exalted habitué of the periphery of the Oval Office or the State Department's sacred seventh floor.

You have another mission, provided no one is allowed to bypass you. You cannot cure, but you can mitigate, the damage that flows from the administrative disarray that is built into our government—partly because of its size and partly because of the egos of various Washington satrapies, whetted by the trouble-spotting press. If your authority lives up to your title, you can force all agencies and departments, if not to speak with one voice to your host government, at least to speak in the presence of one interpreter: you. If you insist on someone from the embassy being present at all official

From *Newsweek*, May 4, 1981. Reprinted by permission of the author.

conversations, then at least your friendly hosts can turn to you afterward and achieve understanding, if not reconciliation, of the different nuances, emphases or even positions to which they have been exposed by the parade of official American visitors.

So perhaps your insulting questioner, implying your dispensability, can be brought to realize that *because of* the ease of "over the top" or "around the end" communication and travel, the ambassador is *more* important than he (or she) was when the government of the United States had only one department engaged in foreign relations.

There are two other ways in which ease of intercontinental travel and communications have affected the ambassadorial role. The first is the frequency with which untutored American eminences may

---

"So your ancient job of helping Americans to understand your hosts, and vice versa, is made more demanding and more important by the ease with which American movers and shakers can show up in foreign capitals. Like all achievers of success, especially political success, they will insist on seeing the 'headwaiter,' and that is you, excellency!"

---

land on the Prime Minister's or the Foreign Secretary's doorstep. Our federal system, after all, makes candidacy for national legislative office turn on essentially local political issues and struggles. In an overseas post, which is a crossroads, you have a marvelous educational opportunity. Without exception, all the travelers from the House or the Senate whom I met (and I met many more in London than I would ever have met in Washington) were eager for as much briefing as we could give them. Especially if they intended to see Prime Minister Margaret Thatcher, they were (wisely) aware that she does not suffer fools at all, let alone gladly.

This tutorial responsibility of embassies is not limited to the legislative branch. Our Federal executive too—unlike the governments of most other countries—is not staffed from rows of backbenchers or echelons of civil servants who have served long apprenticeship. An embassy has a responsibility for adding an international dimension to official awareness, especially if the visitor comes from an office whose preoccupations are primarily domestic, as most government departments are.

So your ancient job of helping Americans to understand your hosts, and vice versa, is made more demanding and more important by the ease with which American movers and shakers can show up in foreign capitals. Like all achievers of success, especially political success, they will insist on seeing the "headwaiter," and that is you, excellency!

Finally, being an ambassador in an age of instant audio-visual telejournalism adds a whole new dimension of potential misunderstanding. The dramatic personalization of instant history, the lust for squabble and confrontation, the bubbling cauldron of hot tar fed by the leaks let loose by official ego—all these capture the shortened attention span of the televiewer. There is an inevitable tendency to grotesque oversimplification of sensitive, delicate relationships that are always more subtle and complex than the "tube" or the "box" can easily portray. Over and over again you will have to smooth the feathers ruffled by television's unavoidable caricature. You will sometimes wish for a blackout. You will be nostalgic for the day when the ambassador was the principal source of information about the United States.

The battle against the misimpressions inherent in the oversimplification of the televised image never ends. You cannot hope to correct it with the viewing public; but you can, or at least must, try to restore balance—to supply the sense of context for the benefit of journalists, officials and politicians who have a professional interest in what goes on within as well as between our two countries.

So, you *are* indispensable, Mr. Ambassador, not in spite of but because of the frightening impact of instantaneous communication—mass as well as private—and the ability of men of state to be almost everywhere at once.

3

What Does an Ambassador Actually Do?

The question of the desirable qualifications of an ambassador and the related question of where such persons should be found can only be answered in terms of the requirements of the job itself. One of the least understood among significant policy positions, the ambassadorial role embraces diplomacy, management, politics, public education, cultural relations, trade, development economics, a panoply of functions. Some of them seem so basic that they have not changed over the centuries. Others are completely new.

The old function—essentially, to represent one group of people to another group of people—is still fundamental. It goes back to the time when tribes, seeking alternatives to perpetual conflict, sent one of their number to parley with the enemy. The procedures and safeguards for such emissaries, now usually referred to as ''protocol,'' were refined in the Middle Ages, laying the foundations on which modern diplomacy was built. Protocol is never the substance of what a modern ambassador does. It is part of the framework within which he operates.

To answer the question ''What does an ambassador actually do?'' in concrete terms rather than in generalities, we have collected essays from three practitioners and a journalist. **David D. Newsom,** who retired after service as undersecretary of state for political affairs, served as ambassador to Libya, Indonesia and the Philippines. The late **Ellis O. Briggs** was ambassador to the Dominican Republic, Uruguay, Czechoslovakia, Korea, Peru, Brazil, and Greece. His book, *Anatomy of Diplomacy,* from which we reproduce a portion, was published in 1968. **Charles S. Whitehouse** served as ambassador in Laos and Thailand. **Langston Craig** is a pseudonym. We thank Mrs. Ellis Briggs and the *Foreign Service Journal* for permission to reprint.

The Tasks of an Ambassador

David D. Newsom

Not long ago at a dinner, an oil company official turned to me and said, "Just what does an ambassador do when he is not attending parties or writing novels?"

There are few positions of significance in national life that are more misunderstood than that of an ambassador. To most people in the United States the word brings up an image of a social dilettante or a public relations man sent abroad to make friends for the United States. These images obscure the actual task and the importance of that task in today's world.

The interests of the United States today encompass security, international trade, access to resources, financial relationships, aid to developing countries, the protection of our citizens abroad, the cultural and moral expressions of the nation, and the fair and effective presentation of this nation's point of view on regional and global issues.

Whether it be in Rome or Kigali, the duty falls on the American ambassador to preserve and to advance these interests. The task has become more rather than less complicated.

In a multipolar world, in which the United States shares influence on events with former allies and confronts the activities of strong and determined adversaries, the good ambassador has a sense of mission. Washington will never totally define for any ambassador what that mission is or prepare the ambassador for the unexpected. Such circumstances require on the ambassador's part an understanding of the broad outlines of U.S. global and regional policies and a sense of how such policies apply to the ambassador's post.

The objective of an ambassador's mission may be a specific goal, such as the renegotiation of an agreement or the release of an American from jail. It may be to correct misapprehensions of U.S. policy or to establish an understanding of a new direction.

The ambassador must give guidance to senior staff members representing several agencies and mold their efforts into a concerted program. Presidential letters give such authority to ambassadors, but with agency representatives depending for their future on Washington evaluation rather than on that of the ambassador, the task of direction must be exercised with diplomatic skill. The task embraces not only relationships with civilian agencies, but an appreciation for and an ability to work with military representatives and to understand their respective responsibilities.

Ambassadors of the United States, wherever they may be stationed, are symbols of a powerful nation. Their intelligence, their perception, their sensitivity, their ability to communicate, and their demonstrated knowledge of the United States project a credible interest in the country of assignment that is helpful to their mission and to their country. If these qualities are absent, the influence and the image of the United States suffer. Few who have not served abroad realize the degree to which those in other countries look to the person of the U.S. ambassador for indications of the seriousness with which the United States views relationships with that country.

Of equal importance is the less conspicuous role of the ambassador as an analyst and a forecaster. In today's world events affecting the interests of the United States can erupt in even the most remote places. Subtle shifts in European attitudes can determine the future of our major defense relationships. A change in government in a remote island can change the plan of our naval deployment. A revolution in an African country can affect our access to important materials and products. An ambassador must be prepared to direct his staff and to participate himself in the delicate task of understanding the inner workings of another political structure and, at times, sensing trouble that even the leaders of the country may not yet detect or admit. The role must encompass, also, a skill—even in authoritarian societies—that reaches out to critics and opponents as well as to friendly leaders. There are even cases where the security of the American staff and community (and of course his own as well) depends on the ambassador's ability to communicate with opposition groups.

An American chief of mission must also be a manager. In larger posts this means overseeing staffs that may include more than a thousand Americans and national employees and budgets that can run into millions of dollars. Although amply aided by administrative officers, the well-run embassy is one in which the ambassador takes a personal interest in the efficiency and welfare of the embassy and of the men, women and families associated with it.

In today's world, the effective ambassador is inevitably a public figure, able to deal with the media and to explain to audiences of a different society and culture the objectives and actions of the United States. In an age of rapid communication an unwise statement is not confined to the country of assignment; it becomes instantly part of the material for the nightly news at home.

American communities abroad look to the American ambassador as a counselor and leader, particularly in areas of potential trouble. In such areas, particularly, the U.S. chief of mission has the responsibility for the security of that community, and—in dangerous moments—for making the delicate and difficult determination, when conditions may require, that the community be evacuated. In more normal times, the ambassador will be called upon to make judgments in difficult visa questions, in conflicts between local laws and the rights of U.S. citizens, and on the conduct of individual members of the U.S. community.

"The ambassador must give guidance to senior staff members representing several agencies and mold their efforts into a concerted program. Presidential letters give such authority to ambassadors, but with agency representatives depending for their future on Washington evaluation rather than on that of the ambassador, the task of direction must be exercised with diplomatic skill."

The successful chief of mission will be sensitive to the needs of citizens whether resident in the country or visiting. This will include congressional delegations, businessmen, media representatives, academics, clergymen, and a variety of persons that will pass through the embassy. The day is long past when a Foreign Service officer regarded his day as spoiled when an American citizen came in with a problem. The Foreign Service is no longer a place for expatriates in spirit.

In a highly competitive world, commerce has become a significant element in the implementation of foreign policy. While the line between the role of business abroad and the functions of U.S. embassies may still be obscure, a competent ambassador will have a sense of the importance of U.S. business abroad and will be alert to both its problems and its opportunities. Where no precise guidelines exist an American ambassador with judgment and initiative willing to act without instructions is often in a unique position to preserve significant U.S. private interests.

Beyond commerce the economic currents can determine the direction of policies and politics. Today's ambassador requires at least a basic understanding of international economics and finance and the significance for the U.S. of local trends and events. In missions in the developing world this includes a sensitivity to the needs of development and to how the limited assistance of the United States can fit realistically and effectively into a broader program.

Besides these general tasks individual posts will bring special problems, such as acts of terrorism, dealing with the narcotics trade, resolving fishing disputes, or the historic residue of a previous colonial presence. The competent ambassador is alert also to these less customary issues.

In a country long accustomed to the image of an ambassador as a man or woman in evening clothes, sipping a drink under a crystal chandelier, it is difficult to move away from a concept that anyone competent to "make friends" and "close to a President" can carry out effectively the role of the President's representative. If such appointments are the norm, the United States can pay a price in at least three ways.

1. *Respect:* Others are quick to see the shortcomings of an American representative and to judge the attitude of the United States accordingly.

2. *Access:* The ability of an ambassador to gain entrée to senior officials abroad is the key to success. That access is less likely to be granted to an ambassador seen as unable effectively to discuss or to represent not only the issues at hand but broader global and regional matters. A high grade support staff can only go so far. In a rank-conscious world a deputy cannot substitute and gain the attention of heads of state and heads of government to the degree possible by a respected and knowledgeable ambassador.

3. *Shift of communication:* The result of a lack of access and effective communication in the field is likely to be a shift of the discussion of major issues to Washington. This has serious potential disadvantages, whatever may be the competence of the foreign ambassadors in the United States. Washington views will be transmitted through one channel. Distribution of those views at the other end may well be determined by that channel. In an assessment of a

situation and of reaction to U.S. policies abroad Washington's view will, in such circumstances, be deprived of the invaluable insights that come from an ambassador on the spot able to circulate with respect and sensitivity at the highest levels of another government.

In a world in which U.S. interests are not taken for granted and need constantly to be reasserted, the men and women chosen to lead our missions abroad today need to be qualified to undertake a task of great variety and frequently of great complexity. Whether they come from a professional core or from private life, they should be chosen not on the basis of an image or a debt but on the basis of their competence to protect and advance this country's interest.

A Day with the American Ambassador, or What Makes an Embassy Tick

Ellis O. Briggs

There is no such thing as a Typical Embassy. Therein lies some of the charm of diplomacy for professional diplomats, as well as some of its frustration. An Ambassador's life can be one of infinite variety, but what is effective procedure at Post A may have little relevance to operations at Post B, in a different continent. Or even at Post C on the same continent. The successful ambassadorial approach in one country may have to be abandoned in the next, where a whole new set of ground rules may be in operation.

Moreover, an Ambassador, to a degree not approached by an executive of comparable responsibility in any other profession, can be at the mercy of forces over which he exercises little control—his own government, and the government of the country to which the Ambassador is accredited. Thus the host government, especially if it is an Emerging Nation, may suddenly wake up to find its treasury cupboard bare and demand of the Ambassador an X-million-dollar credit, to be available to the Minister of Finance by the following Wednesday. Or the State Department, prodded by an eager American representative at the United Nations, may suddenly cable the Ambassador, directing him to twist the arm of the host government until the latter agrees to vote *yes* on some pending General Assembly item, even though the subject may have no more than marginal importance in the relations between the United States and the Ambassador's host country.

These events occur on weekends, when the Ambassador had planned to go fishing, or to catch up on his sleep, or to visit a hinterland province.

In the case of instructions dispatched by Washington, there is little awareness outside the geographic Bureau of the State Department of the mechanics of compliance abroad. There is no picture in the minds of other Potomac officials of the steps that have to be

From *Anatomy of Diplomacy: The Origin and Execution of American Foreign Policy* (New York: McKay, 1968), Chap. 8, pp. 115–20, 130–36. Reprinted by permission of Mrs. Ellis O. Briggs.

taken by an Embassy on the receipt of a message. Having dictated the phrase "you will accordingly seek an immediate interview with the Minister for Foreign Affairs, requesting an assurance on behalf of his Government that . . ." the task of the Washington bureaucrat is accomplished. He can then go home to his martinis, his backgammon, or his P.T.A. meeting, giving no further thought to the problem generated by his telegram until the Ambassador's reply reaches his Foggy Bottom cubicle.

But except in countries heavily dependent for survival on American bounty, and hence readily accessible to the American representative, getting an "immediate interview" with the head of the Foreign Office can be as difficult as it would be for the Washington representative of the country concerned to see on equally short notice the Secretary of State of the United States—even if the Secretary had not just flown off to attend a SEATO meeting in Canberra.

It may be revealing, therefore, to trace what happens to a message dispatched from Washington over the name of the senior member of the Cabinet, telling an Ambassador to take some kind of action.

The Embassy code clerk, having deciphered the telegram and having spotted the word "immediate," will have alerted the duty officer, noting the time—12:28 A.M.—in his log. But since the message is classified, the clerk will have been unable to describe its contents over the telephone; the duty officer, cursing, will accordingly read it in the code room at 1:30 A.M., as likewise recorded. Correctly refraining from waking up the Ambassador about something that cannot be tackled before daylight, the duty officer will appear at the Embassy Residence with the message at eight o'clock the following morning. He will be invited to share a cup of coffee with his Chief, who is already halfway through the local papers.

Most Foreign Offices do not open until ten in the morning, and the first question is whether the Ambassador should try to get through to a subordinate official before that hour, requesting an appointment with the Minister, or whether the Ambassador should make use of the Foreign Minister's private telephone number, communicating directly with him at home, notwithstanding the Minister's possible hostility to breakfast interruptions.

At that point there come into play factors that cannot be found in a rulebook: the Ambassador's assessment of the importance of the message, and its subject matter, in the scale of issues confronting the two countries. The Ambassador must weigh the message in terms of its impact on the host government. He will have to forecast the response of that government, and calculate how much of his own diplomatic ammunition is likely to be required, in order to produce the assurance demanded by Washington. He must decide whether—in the event that the cost in those terms may be considerable—the favorable reply of the foreign government is really an achievement commensurate with the expenditure of that much effort. (With Foggy Bottom bursting with bureaucrats, and all the bureaucrats supplied with paper, all sorts of messages reach foreign capitals demanding ambassadorial action.)

If he doubts the importance of the current project, the Ambassador can bounce back a message to Washington, setting forth his views and "requesting further instructions"—a gambit too frequent recourse to which can be irritating at home, especially if the majority of the Ambassadors receiving the same instruction act upon it without cavil.

In the case in point, the Ambassador concludes that an issue of substance is involved. The message deals with a proposed international conference on maritime jurisdiction, and the host country, possessing a seacost and with appreciable fishery resources, should not only be interested in the project *per se,* but should be receptive to the views expressed by the United States. The Ambassador accordingly hunts up the Foreign Minister's unlisted phone number (given to him shortly after arrival, when the host government decided that the Ambassador knew his business). The Ambassador holds the receiver in one hand and his second cup of coffee in the other, while the Foreign Minister is wrapping a bath towel around his middle and pushing damp feet into bedroom slippers.

The Ambassador describes the situation set forth in the telegram, compressing it into its salient facts and expressing the belief that the interests of the two governments ought in this case to coincide. He bases the early approach to the minister on the unexpected United Nations action, scheduling with so little notice an Assembly debate on the issue.

After asking several pertinent questions, the Foreign Minister says on consideration that he agrees. He volunteers to cable his own UN representative in the sense desired, adding that he will tell his Ambassador in New York to get in touch with his American colleague. "No trouble, my friend. Your call has saved time for us both. I hope we can always settle our problems so quickly. . . ."

The Foreign Minister then returns to his bath. The American Ambassador, having scribbled his reply to Washington on a yellow pad, dismisses the duty officer and turns to the text of yesterday's White House press conference, received overnight in the Radio Bulletin. Mission accomplished.

The action described has taken place under optimum diplomatic conditions: a smoothly operating American Embassy Chancery with an efficient duty officer, an energetic Ambassador enjoying the confidence of the host Government and sharing a language with the Foreign Minister, and an issue soluble in terms of existing bilateral relations. Such conditions, in the troubled postwar period, are not always in conjunction. In Bolivia, Upper Volta, or Czechoslovakia, where interest in the law of the sea may be somewhat less than incendiary, the response will not be identical with that evoked in Japan, Great Britain, Peru, or Soviet Russia, even though all countries—landlocked or not—have the same vote in the General Assembly of the United Nations.

Furthermore, leaving aside the variety of the responses toward the substantive issues raised by that particular message, the circumstances in which a reply is obtainable can differ even more widely, country by country and capital by capital. The Foreign Minister might be out of town, leaving a Vice Minister unwilling to commit his chief. Or, having been found within the inadequate time limit, the Foreign Minister might wish to consult his Chief of State, or his legislative leaders, and then disappear again, remaining inaccessible, until after the clock has run out. Or the host Government might be going through a period of annoyance with the United States, and hence decline on principle to cooperate. Or the American Ambassador might himself be out of town when the telegram arrives, with his Deputy unable within the prescribed period to reach an official of sufficient authority to handle the problem.

All of which is illustrative of the desirability of leaving diplomatic representatives long enough at their posts for them to learn how to operate effectively in the special and distinctive atmospheres prevailing in their respective countries. No two capitals are alike, least of all (for example) the five neighboring capitals of Central America, which share a common language and a common colonial heritage, but in no other particulars resemble each other.[1] . . .

. . . Let us examine how this particular diplomat spends the rest of the day so auspiciously inaugurated.

At nine-thirty the Ambassador reaches his Chancery, having walked the mile and a half from his Residence, to the disgust of the Embassy chauffeur, who can imagine nothing more idiotic than going on foot, when there is a Cadillac automobile to ride in. The first half-hour is spent reading the incoming telegrams, as well as the pink copies of messages dispatched in his name overnight, and in exchanging views with his Deputy, who congratulates the Ambassador on the expeditious disposal of the United Nations matter. Arriving half an hour before his Chief, the DCM [Deputy Chief of Mission] will already have put the Chancery machinery in motion.

"The ambassador must weigh the message in terms of its impact on the host government. He will have to forecast the response of that government, and calculate how much of his own diplomatic ammunition is likely to be required . . . He must decide whether . . . the probable reply of the foreign government is really an achievement commensurate with the expenditure of that much effort. If he doubts the importance of the current project, the ambassador can bounce back the message to Washington. . ."

An informal ten o'clock meeting in the Ambassador's office will bring together the heads of the [Embassy's] five sections, together with the DCM and the CIA representative. Here the day's work is considered, positions adopted, and assignments made. It is the most important meeting of each day, although once a week the Ambassador will have a larger staff meeting in the Conference Room—a sort of weekly summary and orientation session, a principal purpose of which is to tie all the members of the organization together,

---

[1]It is gratifying to report that in contrast to the Roosevelt, Truman, and Eisenhower Administrations, which played musical chairs with American diplomats with such abandon that both furniture and participants were exhausted, and the business of American diplomacy suffered, the average length of ambassadorial service during the 1960s has almost doubled. This has been accompanied by a marked increase in the effectiveness of American representation at a number of capitals.

including Defense and civilian Attachés, newly arrived officers, and juniors getting their first view of how an Embassy functions.

Likewise once a week, the Ambassador will meet with his so-called Country Team, a diplomatic adjunct dear to the heart of Washington which invented it. The Country Team is not a voting organization, but a device to get before the Ambassador the views of the different agencies operating in the country, the progress they think they are making, and the problems they think they are encountering. Participants are encouraged to urge on the Ambassador any course of action they favor, and the Ambassador may or may not go along with those recommendations. When he does not, the matter can be referred to Washington: the subordinate's view, plus the dissenting opinion of the Chief of Mission.

A main objective of the Country Team mechanism is the hoped-for elimination of conflicting reports reaching Washington, a source of never-ending confusion during the 1950s, when non-diplomatic personnel dominated the scene and each agency was the architect of its own floor in the Tower of Babel.[2]

If the Ambassador has a speech to make, he will discuss it at his ten o'clock staff meeting, outlining what he thinks ought to be said, calling for comment, and then assigning to his Public Affairs Officer and to the Chief of the Political Section the responsibility of producing a "first draft" for further consideration. The more experienced the Ambassador, the fewer public speeches he will make, knowing that of the ills afflicting diplomacy, the most painful are those that result from an Ambassador's not keeping his mouth shut. On the other hand, he recognizes that an occasional appearance before a local Chamber of Commerce, and of course shortly after arrival at a new post before the American Society, can represent a useful opportunity to emphasize some pertinent truth or to get across some profitable idea about the work of the mission. Generally speaking, however, the Ambassador concludes that there are too many speeches and too many public statements made by officials abroad, just as there is too much vaporing in the United States by everyone from the President and the Secretary of State down to the smallest sub-cabinet member: the great uninhibited American penchant for sounding off.

------

[2]In some of our larger Embassies, the Deputy Chief of Mission is chairman of all three of these Chancery meetings, thus leaving the Ambassador free to consort with the Prime Minister, to play golf with the heir apparent, and to brood about Larger Issues.

The remainder of the Ambassador's morning will be taken up by appointments. At eleven he receives the Minister for Public Works, an evasive little man who has difficulty in coming to the point, which is the possible availability of credit to finance a dam and accompanying power grid; the Ambassador has present the Chief of the Economic Section and the Treasury Attaché. If the Minister will kindly submit a memorandum outlining the project, it will receive careful and sympathetic consideration.

Encouraged by this reception and impressed by the knowledgeability of the Treasury Attaché about his country's finances, the Minister for Public Works takes his departure, with the Ambassador as a mark of friendly respect accompanying his visitor to the elevator.

Then occurs the first untoward incident of the day. It involves the guardians of the ambassador's outer office, which has been invaded by eight patriotic ladies from Texas, traveling together on a junket, and looking the part. Appearing at the Embassy without appointment but brandishing form letters furnished by their Congressmen, calling upon all comers to take notice, the ladies have been demanding to be received personally by the American Ambassador in order, so the spokeswoman declares, to bear witness.

The aforesaid guardians of the outer office, cognizant of their responsibility to protect the Chief of Mission from such hazards, have just completed a professional brush-off job, only to have it destroyed by the incautious and unexpected appearance in the hallway of the Ambassador himself, recognizable by the ladies even though he has a foreigner in tow and is not speaking English.

By the time the Ambassador is shaking hands with the Minister of Public Works, the eight ladies have surrounded the pair, while the spokeswoman leads her companions in rendering "Deep in the Heart of Texas" with sufficient volume to startle the jackrabbits into Mexico, if not to bring Sam Houston back from his Valhalla.

From the adjacent ambassadorial waiting room this scene is witnessed by the goggle-eyed Ambassador of Rwanda, whose eleven-thirty appointment to make a protocol visit to his American colleague is already twenty minutes past due.[3]

---

[3]In diplomatic practice, a new Ambassador notifies all other Chiefs of Mission of his arrival; thereafter, as rapidly as may be, he calls by appointment upon each of his ambassadorial colleagues. In capitals having large representation, these calls consume much time and are often tedious for the busy American representative, who will, however, incur substantial ill-will unless he is accessible to the representative of even the most implausible nation.

It takes the American Ambassador seven minutes to detach himself from the triumphant Lone Star ladies, and five additional minutes to explain to the bewildered and suspicious representative from Kigali what has happened. Meanwhile, the president of the American Chamber of Commerce, who heads an important American bank in the capital, and who has a twelve o'clock appointment with the Ambassador to discuss a piece of pending legislation, which if enacted might adversely affect American interests, is in turn entertained by the Ambassador's secretary.

Having finally had his talk with the banker, at twelve-thirty the Ambassador, accompanied by the Deputy Chief of Mission, the First Secretary for Political Affairs, and the Defense Attaché, in uniform, depart in the official limousine for the Peruvian Embassy, whose National Day it is. This consumes thirty-five minutes, which are by no means wasted. The Ambassador has a brief talk with the Foreign Minister, who shows him the text of the telegram dispatched to his UN delegate in New York, pursuant to their telephone conversation that morning, and then thanks the Ambassador for his courteous treatment of the Minister of Public Works an hour before—thus discreetly confirming the interest of the host Government in the Minister's dam-and-power project. The Defense Attaché picks up a useful crumb of information from his opposite Polish number, who has been mixing slivovitz with pisco sours and is feeling patriotic. The DCM and the First Secretary, who between them command five languages, cruise about among the guests, exchanging impressions.[4]

At one-ten, the DCM reminds his Chief that he is attending a luncheon at the Italian Embassy in honor of a visiting atomic scientist. They offer a ride to the Dutch Ambassador, and with the glass partition raised, they discuss for the next quarter of an hour various pending NATO matters, plus the latest news from Indonesia.

The Ambassador returns to his Residence at twenty minutes to four that afternoon. He is about to take a short nap prior to the

[4]Since World War II, and especially in the busier capitals, the interminable afternoon receptions to mark national holidays are being replaced by less costly and less painful twelve-to-one stag affairs, to which the foreign Ambassador invites officials of the host Government and members of the diplomatic corps, but not resident nationals, visiting compatriots, or members of the local society. This sensible arrangement results from the multiplication of countries and hence of national holidays. . . . Perhaps the next step may be for the host Government to encourage its diplomatic guests to join forces, on a monthly basis, and offer just one bang-up celebration every four weeks. . . .

arrival of the Economic Counselor and the head of the AID mission, to consider their unreconciled views on a long circular from Washington demanding a study in depth of the relative merits of economic versus military aid on the social structure of the country to which they are accredited, when the DCM telephones from the international airport whither he has rushed to meet an unscheduled Senator, of whose pending arrival the mission has just been apprised by telephone from a neighboring capital. Although it is the height of the tourist season, a suite for the Senator has already been pried out of the leading hotel of the capital by the Administrative Officer. The DCM wants to know whether he should take on the visitor for the balance of the afternoon, or bring him to the Residence for cocktails, or invite him to dinner.

The Senator is not a member of the Foreign Relations Committee. Insofar as the Ambassador and his Deputy are aware, he has no special interest in their country. The Ambassador suggests cocktails at the Residence at six-thirty, with the DCM to convey the Ambassador's greetings and to say he hopes to have a luncheon or a dinner in the Senator's honor, as soon as the Embassy knows the duration of his visit.

The Senator proves to be an affable guest. He leaves the Residence at a quarter to eight, three bourbons the richer and still chaperoned by the faithful Deputy Chief of Mission, and then the Ambassador sits down to a belated family supper, the first he has enjoyed alone with his family in nine evenings, after which he retires to his study with the papers that accumulated in his Chancery desk between his departure that noon for the Peruvian reception and the arrival of the Deputy, Senator in tow, six hours later. Having disposed of the papers, they are returned to the waiting duty officer, successor to the one who called that morning before breakfast, some fifteen hours before.

The Ambassador presently finds himself falling asleep over the latest issue of *Foreign Affairs,* whose writers seem to be getting farther and farther away from center, if not from reality. That night he dreams that eight determined women, wearing sombreros and boots, are punching his chest and pounding his stomach. The Ambassador wakes up, bathed in sweat. He takes a nembutal, and as he drifts off to sleep again, he concludes that somewhere, in some incarnation, there ought to be an easier way to earn a living. . . .

Running an Embassy

Charles S. Whitehouse

Everyone knows what lawyers and doctors do, or policemen and farmers and admirals, but ambassadors are dimly perceived to lead gilded lives in which diplomacy, whatever that may be, consists largely of attending parties and official functions. Obviously the nature of the country in which one is stationed and the scale of American involvement in its affairs (or less often the scale of its influence in the United States) have a bearing on the ambassador's cares, but many general statements can be made regarding the actual daily responsibilities of every ambassador.

First of all he has to see that his embassy functions properly, for even were he a veritable Talleyrand little will be done in a satisfactory manner if his embassy is in a shambles. Now this may sound pretty simple but it is not as easy as it sounds. When an admiral looks across the bridge of an aircraft carrier he sees officers in blue uniforms all of whom belong to the same service. They are all dependent on one Washington department, they all understand their roles very clearly and they are all indisputably under his command. When an ambassador looks around the embassy conference room during his staff meeting there are probably only four or five officers in the room from the State Department: the DCM, the political and economic counselors, the consul general and the administrative officer! The rest are from other agencies and departments: Agriculture, Commerce, CIA, USIA, Treasury. At the largest posts the State Department contingent is many times outnumbered by the rest of the mission. What does this mean?

It means that although the ambassador is armed with a letter from the President affirming his primacy, he is nonetheless commanding a unit whose members have very mixed loyalties indeed and whose professional concerns are often intensely parochial. To make a large embassy function in an orderly well-coordinated fashion and to maintain clear lines of authority and responsibility takes leadership of a very high order; for the mandarins in the mission get directives from their colleagues in their own agencies, and their professional standing—and their promotions—are more dependent on their links with their own agency than they are on anything else. It may seem odd to compare ambassadors to lion tamers, but I have served in embassies in which keeping the big cats on their perches took a bit of doing. While the ambassador can maintain a degree of discipline over his staff, serious inter-agency disputes often require resolution in Washington; but senior officials of the Department of State are not uniformly enthusiastic about doing battle with other agencies, so the ambassador must often exercise patience and sagacity in handling conflicts. In Bangkok when I found that a military intelligence unit had become useless and irrelevant after the end of the Vietnam war, it took half a year's campaigning with CINCPAC* and the Department of the Army (including a trip by the unit's commander from Washington to Bangkok to get me to change my mind) before I succeeded in getting the unit withdrawn.

"It may seem odd to compare ambassadors to lion tamers, but I have served in embassies in which keeping the big cats on their perches took a bit of doing. While the ambassador can maintain a degree of discipline over his staff, serious inter-agency disputes often require resolution in Washington; but senior officials of the Department of State are not uniformly enthusiastic about doing battle with other agencies, so the ambassador must often exercise patience and sagacity in handling conflicts."

In my experience, successful ambassadors met constantly with their staffs and did their utmost all day every day to assure that embassy actions were thoroughly coordinated, by which I mean that they saw to it that mission elements with an interest in a situation or with a role to play in handling a problem were kept informed and permitted to participate intelligently in them. For the ambassador this means meetings, meetings, meetings!

The ambassador's real role, of course, is to represent the United States to the government to which he is accredited, and there are obviously a lot of sides to that. One is that he has to understand that country and that government, and this takes work. It takes study and travel and the ability to be a good listener and hopefully

---

*U.S. military headquarters for the Pacific area ("Commander-in-Chief Pacific")

the ability to remember people and relationships. Most good ambassadors are agreeable and fun to be with, but it is more important to be well-informed and discreet than it is to be charming. In any society there are groups with whom the ambassador should be on good terms. There are his colleagues in the diplomatic corps, the American community, the local government, opposition, intellectual and educational leaders, trade unionists, journalists, bankers, senior officials of the Armed Forces, and the other men and women who are powerful or influential. This is a tall order and you aren't going to do the job if you are a recluse, but you don't have to run yourself ragged either. After several years in Bangkok I learned the back way out of every hotel reception room in which diplomatic events took place and could go through a receiving line, greet some friends, transact a little business with colleagues, whip through the pantry and be back in my car in fifteen minutes. There is no need to stand around for hours sloshing up drinks.

One of the dilemmas in working with foreign governments is how to carry out your instructions. Should you go yourself to the Foreign Minister or perhaps the Secretary General? Should you tip off the Minister of the concerned department ahead of time? Should you send one of your staff instead? Do you want this matter handled discreetly or how generally do you want America's position to become known? In some countries we are involved in significant activities relating to agriculture, public health, oil and gas development, or military procurement. To what extent should the ambassador deal with the ministries concerned? How far can he go without appearing to meddle or creating resentment? I served in several countries in whose affairs the United States was very deeply involved and there were dimensions to diplomacy there which were very unusual indeed. In Laos, for instance, decisions had to be taken constantly on rations for refugees, the rate of American-financed fuel imports, the conditions of service of an indigenous army, the demobilization of tribesmen who had come to depend on us for their livelihood, etc. Admittedly these decisions arose out of very unusual circumstances, but in crisis situations the role of the ambassador often goes way beyond what ambassadors in conventional posts normally do.

Style is not a fashionable concept these days, but there is such a thing as style in diplomacy and it is against the ambassador's handling of matters like these that the professionals in a foreign government and his diplomatic colleagues will judge his performance.

Another little understood question is the degree to which an ambassador can or should use his knowledge, experience and prestige to affect the decision-making process in Washington and try to get the instructions he wants. The rapid communications that are so often believed to reduce the ambassador's stature to that of messenger boy are in fact the tools with which he can exercise influence over policy makers at home. A determined ambassador can use the telephone, letters and embassy cables with telling effect, but this is a difficult and dangerous game in which it is easy to appear to be overstepping one's appropriate role.

One of the things that keeps an ambassador busy is correspondence. The U.S. Government spews out paper at an alarming rate, and to do the job well you have to be able to skim through the unimportant, the press, the periodicals at a great rate and hoist aboard what you really need to know. It is very helpful to be able to dictate with relative ease the innumerable letters, memos and cables which the ambassador has to handle himself even if he has an enormous staff.

Visitors to embassies may find the ambassador relaxed and unhurried, but that indicates only that he has good manners. He has enough to read in his in-boxes and enough work at his desk and enough people to see and enough meetings to attend to keep the most workaholic executive happy, for the calls on his time are never-ending.

"Leisure, Gentility, and Decorum"

A Typical Day of an American Ambassador

Langston Craig

Langston Craig was permitted to make a "time study" of one day of an American ambassador at a large diplomatic post in Asia. The day was a typical one in the sense that it was arbitrarily chosen and the actions and movements of the ambassador were not more numerous or complex than on other ordinary working days. However, some occurrences and problems have had to be slightly modified in order to conceal the ambassador's identity.

"Before you leave, you must sign our guest book," the ambassador said to the distinguished visitor. It was 11:07 a.m.

"You have already given me so much of your time," mumbled the visitor. He signed the guest book and again turned to say good-bye.

"No, no, let me see you to the door," said the ambassador.

As they walked down the spacious stairway of the embassy, and through the hushed quiet of the entrance hall, the distinguished visitor from Philadelphia wondered if the ambassador could be a very busy man. He had given him a half-hour interview in the course of which many of the problems of Khansar had been discussed. The visitor was an industrialist with important connections in Washington, and the State Department had suggested that the ambassador "extend appropriate courtesies."

As his car drove up, the visitor shook the ambassador's hand. "It's been a great pleasure," he said. The ambassador waved as the car drove away. Then he turned and, acknowledging a salute from the Marine guard, quickly walked up the stairs back to his office. It was 11:10 a.m.

When the ambassador returned to his desk, he found there three new notes from his secretary, on top of the pile of the most urgent business. He glanced through the papers, pressed a button, asked to see the economic counselor. Then he turned to examine the draft

From the *Foreign Service Journal,* May 1959. Reprinted by permission.

of a telegram to Washington about the crisis in the Khansar parliament. The secretary came in to say that the economic counselor was waiting. The ambassador asked to have one of the first secretaries of the political section, a young man who spoke fluent Khansarese, stand by. The economic counselor entered. It was 11:19 a.m.

The economic counselor had a problem in connection with the current discussions concerning the sale of certain American surplus agricultural commodities to Khansar. The ambassador listened, asked a few questions, then gave the counselor certain guidelines and instructed him to coordinate with the chief of the political section. Next he received the language officer of the political section to discuss the visit that afternoon of a provincial labor leader who was to call at 2 p.m. Then the ambassador pushed a button to call his social secretary, asked to have inquiries made whether the labor leader, who was in the capital for a few days, was available for dinner the coming Thursday.

The ambassador thereupon resumed reading the draft telegram about the parliamentary crisis. He marked a place where he wished to have more information, had the draft sent with an accompanying slip to the counselor of the political section. He read a secret report about subversive activities in a border province, then signed two letters of thanks to well-wishers who had expressed their complete agreement with the policies of the United States in Khansar. This reminded him of something. He pressed another button. The second one of his personal secretaries entered. It was 11:40 a.m.

"I have to leave now for the reception in honor of the President of Cambria," the ambassador said. "When I return, before lunch, I want to see (he gave the name of another member of the political section) and want to discuss the petroleum scandal. What I want to know is whether (he gave the name of one of the well-wishers) is implicated in this thing. I also want to know whether the press has mentioned yet our negotiation on the agricultural surplus commodities."

The ambassador signed one more letter, a despatch on the forthcoming visit of a productivity mission, and two routine telegrams to Washington. As he left, his secretary showed him an urgent message that had just come in from the American embassy in a neighboring country. As reading matter during his car ride to the reception, the ambassador took along the translations of articles from the local morning press, which had just been delivered to his office.

The reception for the visiting president was an enormous affair. Many distinguished personages of the political, economic and intellectual life of the country were there, as well as all the ranking diplomats of the capital, some of them in resplendent uniforms. There was a leisurely atmosphere of gentility and decorum. The ambassador arrived at 12:10 and, after shaking hands, chatting in apparent relaxation with some of the guests and nibbling a few canapes, took leave from the hosts at 12:27 p.m. Among the guests he was delighted to note the distinguished visitor from Philadelphia.

The visitor from Philadelphia was not quite so delighted. Really, he thought, it seems true that our ambassadors spend all their time at social functions and hobnobbing with polite society.

As the ambassador was waiting for his car to drive up, the minister from one of the neighboring countries came up to him and said: "There has been some trouble at the border. A smuggling affair which may be blown up to distract attention from the parliamentary crisis." The ambassador promised to have a member of his political section get in touch with his opposite number in the minister's embassy that afternoon.

When he returned to the office, the ambassador blew his top.

He asked to see the counselor in charge of the political section and one of the first secretaries. He asked why he had not yet been informed about the border incident. Why did he have to hear of it only at a reception? Had it been mentioned by the government in the course of this morning's parliamentary debate? Who was following the debate anyhow? He asked the head of the consular section to telephone the consul in the town near the border. The political section was meanwhile to check with contacts in the government, the opposition party and the press.

"I want all the available facts by 3:30 p.m., in the form of a draft telegram to Washington, repeated to the American Embassy in (the ambassador gave the name of the neighboring capital)." He asked his deputy chief of mission (DCM) to take up liaison with the local embassy from the neighboring country.

The ambassador had arisen at 6:35 that morning, five minutes later than his usual time. He had read the English-language morning papers over his breakfast coffee, then had bathed, dressed and walked to the embassy where he arrived at 8:02 a.m. At the Embassy chancery, he had found the early summary translations of highlights from the Khansarese morning papers, which had been culled by a team of local translators under the supervision of an American language officer, who had been at work since 6:30 a.m.

The Marine guard had handed him, as usual, an envelope containing the telegrams that had arrived during the night and which had been left by the code clerk when he turned in at 3 a.m. There were eighteen incoming messages, and the confirmation copies of seven outgoing messages of the previous day. One of the incoming messages dealt with the arrival of another group of distinguished visitors from Washington. The ambassador had immediately called his wife to decide what time they could set aside for a reception in honor of those visitors the following week.

At 8:18, the ambassador had discussed the forthcoming social schedule with his social secretary, had reviewed the summary records of two political conversations he had had the previous day, and had asked to see one of the language officers about the parliamentary crisis. At 8:35 he had discussed protocol arrangements for a forthcoming state function. The Dean of the Diplomatic Corps had made a decision, which must be binding on all Chiefs of Diplomatic Missions, but press reports that morning seemed to differ in important respects from what the ambassador had understood. He laid aside five messages and two items from the press translations for discussion at the morning staff meeting. Before going into the meeting, he received the agricultural attaché who was accompanied by an expert on one of the surplus commodities whose sale was being discussed with the local government.

At the morning meeting, attended by the DCM, the heads of the political, economic and consular sections, the service attachés and the heads of agencies attached to the embassy, the ambassador had given a résumé of his talks with two opposition leaders the previous evening. The head of the political section reported about a new trend that had been observed in Communist propaganda addressed to Khansar. An officer of the political section who specialized in Communist affairs had discussed this trend with local public opinion leaders, and the Public Affairs officer was preparing background material to be used by the press attaché in his contacts with local editors and by other embassy officers in their dealings with other Khansarese.

At the meeting, the ambassador had also asked for a progress report on arrangements for the forthcoming trade fair. He asked for a draft schedule for the visit of an important military official who was to arrive the following Monday. He heard an account of the parliamentary crisis, of negotiations for an airline agreement, and the foreign minister's forthcoming trip to the provinces, and gave instructions to have guidelines prepared for use by consular officers if the subject of the pending base negotiations came up in their conversations with provincial opinion leaders.

When he returned to his office after the staff meeting, the ambassador had looked at his watch and found that he still had 40 minutes before the arrival of the distinguished visitor from Philadelphia. He had walked down the hall to the office of the new press attaché and, after asking him how he was coming along, suggested that in future he attend the morning staff meetings. He had then gone to the office of the deputy chief of mission and discussed with him the need to keep up contact with parliamentary leaders especially in view of the present crisis. The DCM was to discuss the matter with the political section and with the service attachés and the heads of other agencies attached to the embassy.

"Seven Deadly Sins" of Ambassadors

An ambassador is, by the nature of his job, subjected to many pressures and temptations. The most successful ones will resist and steer a course away from Seven Deadly Sins:

1. *Parochialism.* Swept away by the persuasiveness and emotions of the capital in which he finds himself, particularly in crisis areas, a chief of mission can become more of an advocate for the host country than for the country that he is supposed to represent.

2. *Head of State Blindness.* The glitter of a court or a presidential palace can feed the myth that to be successful an ambassador must be obsequious to a foreign head of state; and this in turn leads him to shy away from anything that might be displeasing to the local power holders because it might impair the ambassador's "close and cordial relations" with them.

3. *Expatriatism.* The "I am here to deal with the people of the country" syndrome leads some chiefs of mission to look upon the advent of fellow citizens in their domain as an unwelcome intrusion—forgetting that such citizens are, in the last analysis, their only real constituents.

4. *Isolation.* Some believe they can most effectively survey the scene in the host country and stay out of trouble by not venturing beyond the

Then something had gone wrong. The draft plan for the visiting productivity mission, which had been approved by all section chiefs and was due to be sent to Washington in the diplomatic pouch that was being sealed at noon, had been improperly typed up and lacked a paragraph that the ambassador had specifically wanted inserted.

The ambassador had glowered at his secretary. She knew that there was no sense telling the ambassador that it wasn't she who had made the mistake. *Somebody* had made the mistake, and the ambassador's anger was a message she was expected to convey, tactfully but clearly, to the one responsible.

"I want to see this again before it goes out, but it must get into today's pouch," he said. It had been 10:21.

While his principal secretary hurried off, the ambassador had called in the second stenographer and dictated to her a letter to a high official in the Department of State in Washington, on an aspect of the military base negotiations that could be misunderstood by the neighboring country. The letter was to be typed up in draft, with two carbon copies, to be shown to the DCM and the head of the political section, for any comments or changes that they might propose.

---

chancery and the residence, avoiding contact with all but the elite. That path leads to surprises and disaster.

5. *Aimless Aimiability*. An ambassador is never "off the job." Entertaining guests without an objective related to the task brings little advantage and should not be at the taxpayers' expense. He or she who goes abroad to give parties aimlessly and leaves the "substance" to the staff might as well have stayed at home.

6. *Absenteeism*. On the other hand, the chief of mission who wants only the title and prefers to spend most of his time away from his job, perhaps in Florida or California, will be of even less value to the nation.

7. *Skewed Reporting*. The temptation is strong to tell the capital less than it may need to know—to protect budgets, to avoid creating alarm, or to create a positive image of mission and country. This is, perhaps, the shortest path to sudden unfortunate turns and a loss of credibility.

On his or her own at the end of a fragile tether of communication, the ambassador has no easy task. It will be no easier if these most serious pitfalls are avoided, but the task is more likely to be successfully accomplished.

—David D. Newsom

At 10:31 a.m., the ambassador had called in his personal assistant to review with him what that young man was to say to the American ambassador to another country who was touching down briefly at the airport en route to another capital. The personal assistant was to meet the plane, convey the ambassador's greetings and tactfully ask a question about the forthcoming wedding of one of the embassy's best secretaries who was expecting to become the bride of a member of the other ambassador's staff.

The private telephone had then rung. At the same time the secretary opened the door to announce that the visitor from Philadelphia had arrived. At the same time the other door had opened and the social secretary came in with a stack of papers. Standing behind the visitor from Philadelphia was the DCM who, with studied nonchalance, was reading a paper that he obviously wanted the ambassador to read before he closeted himself with his visitor. It had been 10:37.

The ambassador had opened the door wide, stretched out his hand, and had gone to meet the distinguished visitor.

"Delighted to see you! Please come in."

At the same time, he had motioned his deputy into the room and glanced at the paper while asking his visitor to sit down. Meanwhile, the secretary had told the telephone caller (who was the ambassador's wife) that he was in conference, and the social secretary had deposited on the ambassador's desk his personal mail, a list of requests for appointments and a schedule of forthcoming appointments. After briefly studying the secret document that the DCM had brought him, which dealt with opposition plans to bring up the base negotiations in their next attack against the government, the ambassador gave some guidance to his deputy, then closed the door, picked up a box of cigarettes and offered them to his visitor. Then he settled down more comfortably in the easy chair near the visitor, giving him his undivided attention.

An atmosphere of leisureliness, gentility and decorum prevailed in the office. The ambassador, after exchanging pleasantries, began to sketch out the political situation for his visitor.

After attending a luncheon in honor of a visiting trade delegation, where he introduced the guest speaker and chatted with officials of the Ministry of Trade and the local Chamber of Commerce, the ambassador returned to the office to find his deputy waiting for him with news about the alleged border incident. It had been a false alarm. The visiting provincial labor leader, who had arrived at the embassy ahead of schedule at 1:53, was being engaged in conversation by a language officer of the political section who would join the meeting as interpreter.

The labor leader emerged from the ambassador's office at 2:40 p.m., was asked to sign the guest book, was escorted down the stairs by the ambassador, seen into his car, waved off in farewell.

At 2:44, the ambassador started reading the accumulated messages and memoranda on his desk, returned the call of his wife which he had been unable to answer in the morning, then asked to see the administrative counselor to discuss the embassy's finances for the rest of the fiscal year in the light of a recent budget cut. He sent word to his division chiefs that he would be leaving the embassy early that afternoon and must have outgoing telegrams and despatches for signature prior to 5:30 p.m.

A 3:21, he received a telephone call from the minister of the neighboring country, confirming that the story of the border incident had been a mistake.

At 3:26, he received an oral report about the parliamentary crisis, then discussed with the political counselor the award of a medal to a local dignitary, reviewed a draft telegram about Khansar economic problems, signed a telegram to the U.S. Delegation in New York on the probable attitude of the Khansar delegation in the Fourth Committee of the United Nations General Assembly; a letter to a provincial governor asking whether he might visit his province the following month; a note appointing the U.S. representative to an arbitral tribunal; and a despatch about Khansar trade with certain Communist countries. He spent some time reviewing a draft reply, prepared by the political section, to a letter from an official in the State Department discussing a jurisdictional dispute which might require the ambassador's personal intervention with the Khansar government. Then he dictated a despatch about certain diplomatic aspects of the visit of the President of Cambria, on the basis of information he had obtained that morning, had cross-checked at the luncheon meeting, and had confirmed by one of the first secretaries who had been in touch with the Khansar foreign ministry. By that time, it was 4:22.

The ambassador now turned to the personal mail that had been sitting on his desk since the morning. It contained three letters from friends, announcing that friends of theirs would soon be stopping by on trips around the world, and would the ambassador be good enough to receive them? There were also two letters from members of the U.S. Congress, one of them announcing two visits by prominent constituents.

The press attaché came in to inquire whether a press release should be issued on the visit of the distinguished visitor from Philadelphia. (The answer was no.)

The secretary brought in four more incoming telegrams; a photograph to be inscribed as a present for a meritorious local employee who was resigning after many years of service at the embassy; three letters ready for signature, addressed to provincial governors, thanking them for courtesies extended during the ambassador's last field trip which had taken him to their provinces; a report about subversive activities among Khansar students; the afternoon "press highlights" in translation; a secret circular telegram from Washington; two translations of local magazine articles; two memoranda of conversations between language officers and local politicians; a new diplomatic list; a draft memorandum recording his conversation with the labor leader; a telegram on the airline negotiations.

The ambassador asked his secretary to make a dental appointment for him for the coming Saturday. It was 5:45.

After reading and signing more outgoing messages and conferring with his deputy chief about the parliamentary crisis and some personnel problems within the embassy, the ambassador left the embassy chancery at 6:10 p.m. or about twenty minutes earlier than usual, because he had to go home to change before attending a reception at the Embassy of Cambria, again in honor of the visiting President. He arrived at the reception at 6:58 p.m. accompanied by his wife.

The reception was a brilliant affair. Most of the wives of the diplomatic guests wore their best cocktail dresses, some of the military attachés had come in their most resplendent uniforms, some of the guests wore dinner clothes in anticipation of still more formal functions later in the evening. Many of them addressed each other as "Your Excellency" and some were addressed as "Your Highness." Again, there was an atmosphere of leisure, gentility and decorum.

The ambassador and his wife moved among these guests, chatting, drinking, nibbling, nodding, paying casual compliments—when they noticed, in a corner of the room, the distinguished visitor from Philadelphia.

The visitor had been surveying the scene for some time, with a mixture of fascination and suspicion. He strongly sensed that any typical, red-blooded American was very likely to be hoodwinked and bamboozled by this crowd of suave, oily, posturing foreigners. He shook hands with the ambassador, but could not help recalling a book that he had recently read, in which the authors had pointed out that American diplomats should mingle more with the people, far away from the capitals, rather than with politicians and bureaucrats who run the countries and make the decisions.

Somehow, the visitor felt, he had found confirmation of this view. It was quite obvious to him that the ambassador himself was hopelessly caught up in the cocktail party circuit. The ambassador was a nice fellow, he felt, and quite capable in his way. But he was obviously enmeshed in diplomatic formalities and far removed, poor fellow, from the realities of Khansar.

The evening happened to be the only one of the week when the ambassador dined at home without guests. He and his wife arrived at the embassy residence at 8:11 p.m., and after dinner chatted a while together. Then the ambassador again looked over his personal mail and got down to the magazines and newspapers from the United States which had been accumulating for many days.

The ambassador went to bed unusually early that evening, at around 10:15 p.m. He took with him a book that had just been sent by a friend in the United States and which dealt with problems of American diplomats in certain countries of Asia. In that book, the ambassador read with great interest that the really useful ambassadors of the United States play the harmonica, wade through rice paddies and lead guerrillas in the boondocks, instead of living the life of leisure, gentility and decorum that outsiders can so easily observe.

4

An Examination of Requirements and Qualifications

We have invited some outstandingly successful and meritorious foreign diplomats to give their views on requirements and qualifications in order to allow a broader perspective than that of only American diplomacy, and because of course foreign diplomats are also in a good position to comment on the effectiveness of American diplomacy. (Except for one instance these authors are too circumspect to make any critical remarks, but from their definitions of requirements one can deduce where they might think some American diplomats to be wanting.)

Karl Gruber was Foreign Minister of Austria for nine years and his country's ambassador to the United States (twice), Spain, Switzerland and the German Federal Republic. **François de Laboulaye** was French ambassador to Brazil, Japan, and the United States. **Jean Laloy,** his co-author, is a distinguished French diplomat and academician, member of the Institute *(Académie des Sciences Morales et Politiques)* in Paris. Among positions held by **Egidio Ortona** have been Permanent Representative of Italy to the United Nations, Secretary General of the Ministry of Foreign Affairs, and for eight years ambassador to the United States. **Hideo Kitahara** was Japan's ambassador to the Republic of Vietnam, representative to the UN agencies in Geneva, and ambassador to France. **Lord MacLehose of Beoch** (formerly Sir Murray MacLehose) was British ambassador to the Republic of Vietnam and to Denmark and then for eleven years British governor and commander-in-chief at Hong Kong. [The views of two other outstanding foreign diplomats, Berndt von Staden and John G.H. Halstead, are featured in Chapter 2 above.]

Common Denominators of Good Ambassadors

Karl Gruber

Having been both foreign minister and ambassador, I have seen the problem of ambassadorial appointments from the side of both those who make the appointments and those who receive them. I have been in a position to judge when and how ambassadors fall flat on their face, and why some distinguish themselves. I believe there is one common denominator for the performance of superior ambassadors, and that is skill in communication. It is communication of a very special kind, which must be learned, but without the basic aptitude for communication an ambassador cannot be successful in his manifold tasks.

Contrary to the traditional image of an ambassador as a highly polished individual who is so circumspect in what he says that it requires a special talent (allegedly found only in other diplomats) to figure out what he is communicating, I have found that plain speaking is an essential ingredient for a diplomat's success. He must of course be tactful and sometimes artful in the way he communicates, but the message must come through clearly and precisely. Articulateness in explaining, reporting, defending, and discussing information on his country's position and other matters is, to my mind, essential.

The finest among American ambassadors with whom I have had dealings were Robert Murphy, Charles E. Bohlen, G. Frederick Reinhardt, and Llewellyn E. Thompson. They all had a thorough knowledge of international affairs, they were cosmopolitan and had empathy for the concerns of other countries, and they were not too cautious in the way they explained what was going on and what their country was trying to accomplish. The worst among American diplomats whom I have met—and I would rather not give their names—were those who were exceedingly cautious (not merely circumspect) and who wanted to elicit information without giving anything in return.

For communication among diplomats is a two-way street: one cannot expect to obtain much information unless one is able and willing to convey information. The ambassador with whom everyone wants to talk is the one who is interesting to talk with. This was especially true, I think, of the men whom the United States sent out to foreign countries in the earliest days of the republic, when they were statesmen who had been among the decision makers in their own capital and "men of the world" who moved easily among the decision makers of other countries.

"Experience teaches us that the higher the summit the flimsier the agreements. Top-level politicians are much too impatient to watch details, important as they may be, and are always in a hurry to shake hands to mark a 'rapprochement' or other agreement. As an American diplomat once said to me: On an icy summit there grows only what you have carried up there. So it is wise to send conscientious, publicity-shy individuals ahead to prepare the texts and give the top officials concise information about the points to be especially watched.

It will be seen from the above that I am not necessarily critical of the custom of the United States to choose some people for ambassadorial positions who are not professional diplomats—but I believe such persons must have unusual stature in order to be successful, they must be well-read, well-spoken, they must have a thorough knowledge of international affairs, and they must be persons of cosmopolitan tastes and attitudes. Provincialism, ethnocentricity, inability to understand nuances in foreign countries, and the belief that one's own country is the best in everything—these are handicaps which, after a certain age, no amount of training or experience can overcome.

In my own country, which has a relatively small foreign service with only a limited intake of new officers every year, almost every diplomat can expect to become an ambassador. This has its advantages and disadvantages. Among the advantages is that our diplomats need not be afraid that their career will be in ruins if they make a mistake, and that they can consequently be innovative. Among the disadvantages is that there is too little selection of the best people and a consequent tendency on the part of some of our ambassadors to become bureaucratic. Yet excessive competitiveness can also be a liability, as I have seen in the case of diplomats who came from an environment where they had to claw their way to the top: they became competitive also with their peers, both within their service and with their diplomatic colleagues of other countries. Diplomacy requires effective habits of cooperation.

The best ambassadors I have known have been people who, in addition to a thorough knowledge of their own country and the country of their assignment, also have a well-rounded view of the world *(Weltbild)* into which what was happening could be fitted. Without such a world picture it is virtually impossible to reach a firm conclusion about the significance of developments. Nowadays politics permeates every field of state activity. Any small war anywhere has the potential of leading to a world conflagration. The growing closeness and interdependence of nations and the interaction of their public opinions have had the result that the acid of ideological indoctrination seeps into every cleft of international and internal differences. No wonder that any cool assessment of the moving forces of our times requires increased knowledge, sound judgment, and the ability to attach the proper importance to what is happening in a large variety of fields. A good ambassador must understand the significance also of things that happen outside the area where he is accredited.

Communication, as I have used the term above, includes not only collecting and conveying information to and from one's government; it also means negotiating both in the sense of developing concrete agreements and in the sense of adjusting differences and lining up support outside of concrete agreements. While skillful reporting makes the reputation of the ambassador, negotiating is the real essence of his activity. Negotiating is not just sitting at a table where two or more countries more or less oppose one another. It begins a long time before a date is set for sitting down at the table. The process of softening up the other side is almost as important as the exchange of more or less brilliant arguments at the negotiating table.

The ambassador must convince the other government of the importance of the subject under negotiation, and of a compromise useful to his own country. But he must also convince his own government of the limits within which a compromise can be found (or even whether a compromise is necessary). People at home are often inclined to consider the limits recommended by an ambassador as due to excessive caution on his part, alienation from his own country, or plain muddleheadedness. The worst thing would be to recommend or predict an outcome of the negotiations which turns out to be too pessimistic, for instance if the foreign ministry then sends out someone "stronger" who finds that he could "easily" obtain more than the ambassador had thought possible. To find the right course between these conflicting assessments needs skill, experience, courage, and a cool head. The least desirable outcome from the effort to steer between the Scylla of failure and the Charybdis of over-cautiousness would be to send meaningless communications to the home office "in order to protect oneself." One may protect himself or herself for the immediate moment but may damage his further career in the process.

A good diplomat must be precise. Experience teaches us that the higher the summit the flimsier the agreements. Top-level politicians are much too impatient to watch details, important as they may be, and are always in a hurry to shake hands to mark a "rapprochement" or other agreement. As an American diplomat once said to me: On an icy summit there grows only what you have carried up there. So it is wise to send conscientious, publicity-shy individuals ahead to prepare the texts and give the top officials concise information about the points to be especially watched. For instance, the word "support" can mean anything from a timely smile to substantial military support. Specificity is therefore most important. Naturally there are exceptions when agreement for the sake of agreement, even at the cost of vagueness, is desirable or necessary—but such cases are very rare.

A good diplomat also needs a sense of humor. He should always have some remarks ready to ease tension once negotiations get near a breaking point. One example that comes to mind involves a negotiation in which everything went wrong. (It happened to involve agrarian exchanges in Central Europe, a subject that is always tough and intractable). One of the negotiators had a long beard, and his stolid demeanor did not augur well for a successful outcome. His counterpart finally said: Before we part, I have one more question. When you go to sleep at night, do you tuck your beard under the covers or do you leave it above them? There was laughter all around, and for the first time the patriarch allowed a smile to crease his lips. Eventually an agreement was concluded, actually a lot sooner than had been expected. I do not mean to imply that the jocular question was the reason for the successful outcome of the negotiation, but I believe the incident illustrates the importance of the ability to loosen up the atmosphere, of knowing when some levity will help smooth the way to easier discourse and thus to agreement.

A word about discretion. An ambassadorial position should never be given to anyone who is hungry for publicity. In my opinion it is best, even in official reports, to use personal quotations only when absolutely necessary, unless the information conveyed is meaningful only when attributed to a certain high-ranking functionary who conveyed it with attribution in his mind. If ever a "friend" or mere acquaintance reads his name in a report of another government, even if everything in that report is favorable to him, he is much less likely to be candid and open at the next encounter. Any experienced diplomat knows that written reports nowadays can find their way to offices for which they were never intended. To give contacts confidence that their remarks will be held in confidence, I usually preferred to talk with them in informal surroundings rather than in their offices. I also found it prudent even to protect my handwritten notes.

Finally, like anyone who wishes to be successful in a competitive environment, an ambassador must have good judgment. This goes almost without saying, but good judgment today doesn't mean what good judgment meant at the time of sailing ships and horse-drawn carriages. When important things are happening, the ambassador's interpretation of them must be prompt if it is going to do any good because the press will be doing its own interpreting and so will other governments. Therefore reporting and analysis must sometimes be not only timely but almost instantaneous. Good judgment today must come faster than it did a generation ago. And if an ambassador has in his mind a concept of the interrelationship between events around the world, he is more likely to be listened to and his judgments will carry greater weight. This applies both to his written communications to his capital and his oral exchanges with officials of the country to which he is accredited.

Qualifications of an Ambassador

François de Laboulaye *and* Jean Laloy

The first reaction of most professional diplomats, when they are asked about the criteria to be used in choosing ambassadors, is to describe their own qualifications. This is a very natural reaction, but if anything useful is to come from such an inquiry it is necessary to step back and look at the essential elements of the position of chief of mission, i.e., of ambassador.

One simple definition of diplomacy is that it is the *oral* aspect of international relations. There is an essential difference between what is written and what is spoken, not only because spoken words are essentially more ephemeral *(verba volant),* but because the spoken language has infinitely more nuances, being both richer and more subtle than written texts.

Consequently, in an oral exchange one can suggest more than one could in writing, and if one knows how to listen can also understand the other side better. It is in the oral domain that not only ''interests'' can be adjusted or comprehended, but also viewpoints, plans and intentions. But oral diplomatic communication can only be effective if the conversations are part of an ongoing process, if the talks stretch over a period of time and can be resumed each time when it is necessary. And such conversations will only be effective if the interlocutors, while of a level of responsibility, are not those who hold supreme responsibility. If the top people meet face to face, men or women whose every word risks being the last word, the word without further recourse, most of the time they will not say anything useful because the tension is simply too great. On the other hand, someone who is situated a little lower on the ladder of responsibility can orally explore things much further without compromising anyone but himself, and in this manner he may encounter opportunities which he may either seize or let slip by.

No telephones, certainly not a red or green one, can change the situation. They have their utility in certain cases but they do not do away with the necessity for permanent conversation which, in the strictest sense of that term, is diplomacy. This is how we look at the essential requirements of the position. Let us now look at how and from where it may best be filled.

It seems to us that even with the most rigorous selection a corps of the highest ranking diplomats will not consist only of superb performers. Let us be honest—nobody has to the same degree all the qualities necessary to be a perfect ambassador. The distribution among them is likely to be the same as elsewhere: ten percent who are very good and the rest less good, some of them still less so. It would be a great mistake to seek only one type of personality. Yet there are certain qualifications which strike us as essential.

One qualification is what a French colleague, who is now a well-reputed author, called "the specialty of the general." The ambassador must always have his eye on the most general aspects of what he does, namely on the overriding interests. These of course today cover fields which are more and more specialized: not only strategy and tactics, economics, technology, but also social relations, pure science and, finally philosophy, culture, and religion.

What, then, is to be done? One has to supply the ambassador with attachés or special advisors. What then will be his relationship with them? Either he has confidence in them and delegates his authority, in which case he may rapidly lose control of the operations, or else he will not rely on them but will not be able to tell what is to be done. It is, therefore, highly desirable that he should have his own judgment which comes from experience. What kind of experience? Experience that comes from success in previous operations. In other words, it is not a bad idea that the ambassador should have had in his private life occasion to come to grips with the "real world" and that he should know, in any case, the colossal inertia of social structures and of individuals. In this manner he should be able to judge the quality of his advisors and experts and draw profit from their advice. It is true that he must also have a certain amount of technical knowledge in order to properly appreciate the quality of that advice. We believe that frankness requires us to state that there is no neat solution to this dilemma. There is no perfect way out. And there is no perfect ambassador. If there were such a person he would be highly inconvenient and bothersome.

In addition to the enlargement of the domains of science and culture which makes it difficult to discharge the functions of an ambassador during these closing years of the century, there are other problems which have to do with the transformation of the very tissue of international relations.

There was a time when it was enough to defend the "national interest," which was defined as everything that contributes to the prosperity, autonomy and prestige of the society and the state which is represented by an ambassador. There was no problem; it was understood that the purpose was to maintain the equilibrium between the five or six leading powers and at the same time to obtain commercial advantages, obtain respect for the rights of one's nationals, for one's flag, etc. Everyone's horizon was limited to his own nation. *"Wer von Europa spricht,"* said Bismarck, *"hat unrecht"*—whoever speaks of Europe goes beyond what is his business. Put in simple words, whoever used themes that spoke of Europe was doing so only for selfish national reasons. That was perhaps true in 1878; it certainly is not true in 1983.

"It should go without saying that there are strict limits, dictated by common sense and the realities of the situation, to how far an ambassador can go in opposing a position of his own government. If a compromise is not possible and once the final decision has been made, he must of course loyally and scrupulously implement it even if it goes against what he had recommended. But until the final decision is made an ambassador owes his government the frankest and most unvarnished advice."

Today the horizon of diplomacy has widened under the influence of the threat of universal destruction, the growing interconnection of economic interests, the vast movements of populations, the diffusion of technical knowledge, the influence of the media, etc. Today, therefore, one has to take account both of national and of collective interests, which means that an ambassador must be alert to the effects that the policies of his government may have on others. Unless he is able to encompass both the national and the collective dimension, he is not doing his job properly. In a sense he cannot intelligently defend his nation's interests, for these encounter the interests of others everywhere. There are of course ambassadors who maintain a narrow perspective, but they are not really effective and thus do not belong to the minority of good ones.

His position, being situated at a high level of responsibility without himself having the power to make political decisions, allows the ambassador to weigh the national interest against the universal interest and to throw his weight into the scales of the latter if that is necessary. Of course this entails the risk of making himself odious to his own government or to the host government or to an international organization to which he may be accredited—or to all three at the same time.

Here, again, one must not expect a perfect solution; there can never be a stable equilibrium. What is essential is that the two concerns, the national and the collective one, be clearly understood and recognized at all times. In this the character—the strength of character—of the chief of mission plays an important role. He must not be narrowly centered on his own country. He must always seek to understand the reasons that dictated policies of his own government as well as those of the government of the host country.

It happens occasionally that an ambassador is accused of representing the interests of his own country less effectively than he represents those of the country to which he is accredited. Of course an ambassador does not like to hear this. And yet, without indulging excessively in paradox, it might be said that the accusation constitutes, at least in part, also a tribute to the intellectual and moral qualities of the diplomat in question.

It should go without saying that there are strict limits, dictated by common sense and the realities of the situation, to how far an ambassador can go in opposing a position of his own government. If a compromise is not possible and once the final decision has been made, he must of course loyally and scrupulously implement it even if it goes against what he had recommended. But until the final decision is made an ambassador owes his government the frankest and most unvarnished advice. In some cases, if he finds it incompatible with his conscience to implement what he believes to be a wrong decison he can of course resign—but such cases should be rare.

There remains the question where one should look for good ambassadors, whether they should be professionals or persons drawn into diplomacy from outside. It is difficult to be categorical: some professionals have turned in amateurish performances, and there are cases where amateurs rather quickly became good professionals. Yet one should not underrate the existence of a "diplomatic technique" which may seem esoteric to outsiders but really bases itself on long experience. There are real problems if one seeks to enrich the diplomatic establishment with talented outsiders from the world of business or finance or education; but those problems would be greatly diminished if the movement went in both directions—if there were a system of rotation whereby career diplomats go out periodically into that world to do practical work at a high level of responsibility and thus to enrich their own experience—and the diplomatic service—with a better knowledge of the problems of the nongovernmental world. In this manner there would be a greater likelihood of coming up with the desired type: not "specialist of the general" but *specialist and generalist* at the same time, which is not so simple.

The Indispensable Catalyst

Egidio Ortona

It has been observed that in the history of diplomacy the most prominent and effective early manifestations were the reports of the Venetian Ambassadors to the Republic at the threshold of the modern era. A recent thorough study of the state archives of the Republic of Venice show that already in the sixteenth and seventeenth centuries the accurate presentation of political situations was not the main purpose of those reports. The ambassadors used to inform the Doge not only about the political environment and events, but also about concrete and practical economic and social developments like the crop of cereals, the price of gold, the fiscal system, or pauperism in the South of Italy. If assessments in those fields were already the aim of diplomacy centuries ago, how much more is to be expected of diplomats in this day and age!

Today the number of problems which have to be solved by international negotiations is of such magnitude that unavoidably they have to be entrusted to the work of eclectic individuals who must be acquainted more than in the past with finance, banking, trade, energy, armaments, computer technology, etc. The subjects to be dealt with under these headings, long before reaching the stage in which they are debated in negotiations, have to be the object of constant, thorough, exhaustive search and learning. The heads or members of government, in other words the individuals devoted to political activity in their own countries, can intervene only to give the final touch or the political consensus to what has been previously worked out through negotiations. In fact, the increase in commercial and cultural exchange throughout the world, and the ever more frequent meetings between chiefs of governments and other top government officials, do not outdate or diminish the role of a diplomat, but to the contrary, demand of him vaster, more articulate specializations, as well as a deeper application of public relations techniques.

With the multiplication of summit-level meetings (including minister-to-minister meetings), the work of diplomacy certainly has acquired new and augmented responsibilities. Meetings at those levels require meticulous preparation which can be successfully achieved only through the work of technicians in foreign relations. Suffice it to say that a notable part of the work done before such meetings concentrates just on preparation of the "final communiqué," and the agreements and disagreements on that document determine to a great extent how the meeting itself will go. Although the diplomat cannot substitute for the political leaders, he often has to provide for them the knowledge of specific problems that they cannot easily acquire, pressed as they are by their internal political worries or influenced by the demands of press coverage.

". . . When his prime minister or minister of foreign affairs appears in person to deal with the foreign government, the ambassador has the difficult task of 'piloting' the visitors in the foreign environment of which they do not have great knowledge or expertise. . . . The ambassador is there to check, channel, patch up, temporize, catalyze, buffer."

One hears the opinion from time to time that even if ambassadors were done away with, this would not affect the free and full development of political relations, trade and cultural exchanges, because these would be carried on by means of meetings of chiefs of government, of ministers of foreign affairs, of finance, of commerce, of governors of central banks, of representatives of the arts, all of whom could supply periodically the fabric of the necessary contacts. I hope that this can now be seen to be no more than a brilliant paradox. Even if it is true that the margins of action and power of a diplomat are reduced because of the facility with which instructions reach him through telephone or telex, he still has to act very often without instructions, or with incomplete or contradictory ones, and in any case must adapt his instructions to what will be effective with the local government.

Too often when instructions are written at home they are reflective of the domestic political temper and need to be "translated" into something that will yield useful results in the sometimes tricky foreign environment. And when his prime minister or minister of foreign affairs appears in person to deal with the foreign government, the ambassador has the difficult task of "piloting" the visitors in the foreign environment of which they do not have great knowledge or expertise. The most difficult work that a diplomat must perform is to induce the visitor to act both in line with the interests of his own country and, as far as possible, not in contrast with what the host country can accept. Too often even a well-traveled top politician is blinded by national affairs and motivated by party politics at home. The ambassador is there to check, channel, patch up, temporize, catalyze, buffer.

All of what has been said applies to both bilateral and multilateral diplomacy. In the international organizations a deep knowledge of procedural rules provides the means essential to successful activity in that context. According to my own experience, having been both Ambassador to the United States and to the United Nations, the fundamental endowment of the diplomat must be the same in both cases, except for the obvious need in the second case of greater consciousness of international interactions and of the growing needs and collective strength of Third World countries. In both cases an ambassador's task is to harmonize the positions, ideas, approaches of the experts in various sectors of activity, whether they operate in his own mission or come from departments of the central government: He must constantly avoid discrepancies between these various elements so as to produce effective common positions.

While the main elements, characteristics and problems of modern diplomacy are common to all diplomats, there are important differences in the levels of responsibilities, duties and risks between American diplomats and diplomats from other countries. All American diplomats abroad carry a higher degree of responsibility than others, simply because toward every country, friendly or adverse, they project the position of a superpower. A gesture by an American representative can possess more importance, either in encouraging friends or in deterring potential or actual enemies, than a similar move by a diplomat of another country.

At this critical time for the balance of power and alliance systems, an American ambassador should be knowledgeable and steeped in an understanding of past events in other areas in order to integrate a full understanding of the requirements of the present. A deep knowledge of the history, culture, and economy which motivate other countries whatever their size, must become the baggage of American diplomats. Such knowledge manifests itself in the form of respect and objective interest, rather than an attitude of potential interference, the misinterpretation of which is always a risk for a superpower. In other words the American diplomat should be conditioned to avoid any expression of "arrogance of power" and try on the contrary with a deep insight in other countries' complexities to penetrate into their needs and expectations. I would add that the importance of such feelings and attitudes should also be conveyed by American diplomats abroad to the members of congressional committees which often visit foreign countries. In the rigid separation of powers prevailing under the American constitution, I consider essential that representatives of both the executive and legislative branches speak the same language and operate under the same assumptions and with the same approach in dealing with foreign representatives.

The Makings of a Good Ambassador

Hideo Kitahara

When I started my career as a diplomat before the second world war, it was under an ambassador who, to this day, seems to me to typify the accomplished classical diplomat. In addition to Japanese, he knew Greek and Latin and spoke English, French and German. He used to say that in order to perform a diplomat's duties satisfactorily, one always had to be in a position to answer three questions: Who? When? What? The meaning of these three questions is that a diplomat facing any given political move must, under all circumstances, be able to tell his government who made a decision, on what date, and what it was about. This ambassador's threefold question is, I believe, a fair summary of an ambassador's task in the classical era, and of the qualities required to fulfill them. First and foremost, he had to inform his government about the political life in his country of residence so as to ensure proper handling of relations and negotiations between states. Within the framework of their governments' instructions, ambassadors enjoyed extensive representational and negotiating authority. As a rule, inter-state relations were governed by treaties and agreements. International life was conducted on the basis of respect for one's signature: *pacta sunt servanda.*

Today international life and diplomatic relations are completely different. There are many more independent states, and the number of diplomatic missions has grown exponentially. Understandably enough, an ambassador will not do exactly the same work when posted to a superpower as when he is in a country with virtually no land, population or resources. In the days of the League of Nations, the international order was in the hands of a small number of independent states to which were appended the colonial complexes. But in the meantime other forms of interdependence have emerged and have given rise to international legal entities to which diplomats are accredited, as is the case in the European Community, the O.E.C.D., and the United Nations with its many specialized agencies.

An entirely new complex of issues has arisen, involving such issues as the environment, population, science and technology, economic and social development, narcotics, the law of the sea, or nuclear energy—issues of great importance which did not even exist a generation ago and with which a diplomat today must be conversant. Ambassadors accredited to international bodies no longer engage in state-to-state relations but deal with collectivities specializing in economics, international trade, culture, etc. So their competence should be both extensive and highly technical, as they are expected to handle issues involving such matters as non-tariff barriers or EC agricultural regulations.

"(Ambassadors) must certainly strive to promote their country's national interests, but should not follow narrowly nationalistic impulses to which people are subject who have not made international relations their career. A good ambassador must be a patriot—that goes without saying; but he must always bear in mind that every country is part of an international system and that the future of the world depends on at least a tolerably good functioning of that system."

I think it is obvious that this requires an entirely different type of diplomat than those who engaged only in the traditional forms of international relations. The rise of multilateral diplomacy has been accompanied by a rise in rapid and easy international communications. The number of international meetings of heads of states and governments and of ministers has multiplied since the second world war. This trend, sometimes called direct diplomacy, has also substantially changed the role of ambassadors—changed it but not lessened its utility and importance. Politicians and direct government envoys, and non-professional ambassadors appointed on the basis of political criteria, tend to focus on the short term, if not on spectacular action. Professional ambassadors, acting as advisers to them, are responsible for reminding them of the importance of continuity and stability in international relations and for shifting the emphasis to a longer-term view.

Yet another noteworthy feature of modern diplomacy is its organizational complexity. Major embassies house political, military, economic, scientific, agricultural, cultural and other departments. Thus an ambassador's role is also akin to that of a company manager, in charge of sometimes over a hundred staff members. Consequently, an ambassador must be a good administrator.

The qualifications of a modern ambassador are implicit in this brief description of his duties. First, he must have in-depth knowledge and understanding of major world problems. Superhuman capabilities would be necessary for one to be familiar with all the details of these global issues. So ambassadors should try to form a clear picture of the international situation, to analyze it properly and to evolve their own judgment. They can no longer be content with understanding bilateral relations alone, in view of the interdependence of nations. There are far more factors in this judgmental process then there were in the days of classical diplomacy; consequently, the ability to synthesize should be developed even more than the ability to analyze.

As communications were facilitated—thus giving rise to "direct" diplomacy—ambassadors lost a large part of their role as governmental go-betweens. The days when ambassadors awaited instructions and solemnly conveyed messages are over. Modern ambassadors take it upon themselves to inform their governments about the situation in their country of residence, about trends in public opinion, about possible reactions to measures considered by their governments. Often, because of the very speedup of communications that is supposed to lessen their effectiveness, they can suggest to their foreign ministries how they should be instructed. And because the ambassador is on the spot and knows both the issues and what can reasonably be achieved, he (or she) can have more influence than an ambassador had in the days of slower communication.

Thanks to the information that embassies collect and synthesize, ambassadors.thus prepare the ground for and sometimes influence the initiatives of their governments, and are then in the best position to explain these moves in terms that the host country will best understand. This new role of ambassadors requires them to make many new kinds of contacts, not only in official circles but also in all social groups and more particularly in the media. In this way, ambassadors continue to "convey messages," but they convey them to millions of people.

As regards the human qualities an ambassador should have, it seems to me that the principal one is broadmindedness. Ambassadors should be open to cultural diversity and be able to understand it. They must certainly strive to promote their country's national interests, but should not follow narrowly nationalistic impulses to which people are subject who have not made international relations their career. A good ambassador must be a patriot—that goes without saying; but he must always bear in mind that every country is part of an international system and that the future of the world depends on at least a tolerably good functioning of that system.

A Short List of Key Qualities

Lord MacLehose of Beoch

"Don't let it occur again." This concluded my first contretemps with a British ambassador, on the morning after my first dinner in his residence in my capacity as his newest first secretary. "Continentals don't like being nudged towards the lavatory after dinner; it is a purely English custom; why didn't you know?" Clearly my upbringing had been neglected, but I tried to fight back. "But Sir, what about me?" "Well you mustn't and that's all there is to it." The reaction carried me continent through thirty years of diplomatic dinners.

He was an excellent ambassador and did not confine himself to such trivia, but the anecdote illustrates one side of an ambassador's life: whether his embassy is large or small, he is the head of a family consisting of his staff, and he and its senior members must train, drill, direct, rebuke and encourage them so as to make the embassy a smooth-running machine that can be relied on to handle efficiently any situation, however important or however trivial. Consequently a good ambassador must have personality and be a leader, be someone whom it is natural for his staff to look up to, and someone also for whom looking down at his staff in friendship and in collaboration is natural.

In this essay describing some of the key qualities I have seen in successful ambassadors, the list is necessarily short. I have taken for granted the essential minima expected of someone who must work in close contact with national political and commercial leaders and national media, such as experience, grasp of affairs, and facility in the spoken and written word.

The best embassy I served in was in Paris under an ambassador who was a towering personality and natural leader as well as a master of diplomacy. Those of us in charge of sections met him at 9:30 a.m. every morning. We discussed the morning papers, and he told us anything of interest said to him the previous day. On any matter within our province we were expected to give an immediate explanation of what it was all about, or say whom we knew who could tell us, or whom we knew who would not tell us but might tell him, the ambassador. Not to have the facts by 9:30 was bad;

but not to have the contacts that would have them was a cardinal sin. Some ambassadors or their wives treat invitations to their staff like Royal Commands, and prior engagements have to go by the board. However, in that embassy a prior engagement to someone of the country was always an acceptable excuse. The ambassador knew that without those contacts his embassy could not function.

This brings out another aspect of a good ambassador. He must make his staff feel part of a team in which each knows what is expected of him; and to get the best out of the team, he must not only lead it but be part of it himself and not above and remote from it. There is great satisfaction in being part of such a team, knowing that is is equipped to deal with anything that comes.

"Of course it is ruinous to the work of the team and effectiveness of the embassy if the ambassador cannot use its products. He is equipped with entrée to the highest political, commercial and intellectual circles, with a house and servants and allowances to ensure he has easy relations with all who can influence his country's interests; so his staff have the right to expect he will use this paraphernalia, as well as his greater experience, to give point and substance to their work and to discuss with them how this should be done."

Apropos of an embassy team having to be ready to cover all issues of interest and to be clear about who covers what, when I was ambassador to Denmark the British press made a great to-do about the prevalence of sex shops and the degeneracy of youth. Visitors invariably asked about it. "Is something rotten in the State of Denmark?" the bigger bores would enquire. The whole thing struck me as ridiculous, but to keep the visitors at bay I suggested to a young second secretary that the subject should be his. Subsequently, an earnest and humourless mission from the U.K. came to observe this allegedly permissive society, which they were either for or against—I forget which. But at their final press conference they complimented the young second secretary by name on his help and expert knowledge. He took years to live down this kiss of death.

Of course it is ruinous to the work of the team and the effectiveness of the embassy if the ambassador cannot use its products. He is equipped with entrée to the highest political, commercial and intellectual circles, with a house and servants and allowances to ensure he has easy relations with all who can influence his country's interests; so his staff have the right to expect he will use this paraphernalia, as well as his greater experience, to give point and substance to their work and to discuss with them how this should be done. He must be prepared to go out front and do and say what is necessary whether to minister, tycoon or editor, and indeed to relish it. He must be robust. Diffidence never got an ambassador anywhere.

And as he must be robust with the leaders of the country to which he is accredited, so also must he be with leaders of his own country. Ultimately it is his Minister who is master, but the ambassador has and must use to the full, his duty to warn, argue and protest in the light of his local knowledge, as well as to inform, advise and ultimately to act on instructions. But there is no more unpleasant task for an ambassador than to argue on his country's behalf a policy which he believes is unfair or misguided, and nothing is so destructive to an embassy's morale.

So in addition to officials in his Foreign Ministry, an ambassador must get to know the Ministers and the Members of Parliament and businessmen and journalists of his own country who are interested in the country to which he is accredited. To the leaders of that country he carries Letters of Credence asking that he be believed, but it is often just as important to his country's interests that he be believed at home. So it is helpful if in addition he cultivates his personal credibility and even something approaching a power base in interested circles in his own country. Once a Secretary of State went so far as strongly to encourage me to do such essentially domestic political work so as to take some of the pressure off him and his Ministers on a then unpopular cause. So here is another facet of an ambassador: he must be able to operate in the area where bureaucracy, public relations and politics all meet.

When accused of an undiplomatically blunt riposte to President de Gaulle, a British ambassador (and an outstanding one) is credited with replying "Do you want me to be man or mouse, politician or diplomat?" To be good in a hot embassy an ambassador must be prepared to act the politician and publicist at his own discretion and take the consequences. Of course to do this he must have the confidence of his own government and represent their policy accurately, but the method and timing must often be his own. If relations between countries can be dealt with in confidence in quiet rooms, so much the better, but often they cannot be, and the ambassador must be ready to get movement by going public.

In all these activities the ambassasdor must retain the confidence of the government to which he is accredited. When the policies and interests of the sending and receiving states diverge in important respects, it is the ambassador's duty to warn against it and explain the consequences. This usually involves the speaking or writing of disagreeable truths. It is not enough, however, to be truthful—the ambassador must also be believable. He may have to be clear at the expense of being tactful, since he must above all make sure that each government doesn't misunderstand what the other's intentions are, and the ambassador must see that the dialogue is maintained in a way in which it can continue. This task can be appallingly difficult, but personal integrity can carry an ambassador through. Ellsworth Bunker's embassy in Vietnam, and Henry Kissinger's negotiations with both China and the Middle East states are examples of how this problem can be surmounted.

So we have a further facet of a good ambassador—integrity. One who attempts to persuade by overstating his case or who seeks to please by understating problems will eventually lose all credibility, and how often has one seen this happen with the self-appointed unofficial intermediaries who too often muddy international relations!

In conclusion, what about the merits of political as opposed to career ambassadors? Though not infrequent, political appointments are not in the British tradition, but with some notable exceptions they have usually been a great success. But as this essay suggests, to be an ambassador requires special disciplines and a knowledge of dos and don'ts most easily acquired by the long experience that goes with career. Moreover it is difficult for an outside appointee to perform the leadership-of-a-team function that gets the best out of an embassy—though some political appointees have done it with marked success simply because they were that sort of person. And this is the crux of the matter: appointments to important embassies should be made because appointees have the right characteristics to fill the job, either through career experience or other qualifications, but not because they are either career diplomats or politicians.

Nevertheless, a well-run diplomatic service ought to be able to field suitable career candidates for virtually all embassies, though there have been and always will be exceptions. Indeed some of the great names of post-war diplomacy have been political appointees—though so have some of the outstanding failures. However, if political appointments were to become the rule rather than the exception and fill the majority of embassies of importance, the career service would cease to attract or retain the right calibre of entrant, and the country would reap double trouble from inexperienced ambassadors supported by deteriorating staff.

5

The View from the Senate

The United States Constitution (Article II) gives the Senate a role in the appointment of ambassadors by specifying that the President "shall nominate, and by and with the consent of the Senate, shall appoint ambassadors." The responsibility has been lodged in the Committee on Foreign Relations whose recommendations are almost invariably confirmed by the full Senate. The Committee is confronted with a dilemma.

On the one hand there is a feeling that the President, except in very rare cases, should have the prerogative of appointing and sending abroad envoys whom he has personally chosen and who enjoy his personal confidence. This principle has led some to take the position that even if a candidate is unqualified he should be confirmed if no grave fault is found against him. On the same side of the dilemma is the reluctance of the committee to probe systematically for weaknesses in a candidate, which could hold up nominees to undeserved public obloquy in a manner that might discourage persons from outside the diplomatic career from seeking public service.

On the other side of the dilemma is the fact that the Senate has responsibility for seeing to it that candidates are qualified for the assignments they have been given. There is now even a legal requirement (cf. Chapter 9) that individuals assigned to be chiefs of mission "should possess clearly demonstrated competence to perform the duties of chief of mission" and that "contributions to political campaigns should not be a factor in the appointment of an individual as chief of mission." The committee has from time to time raised objections with regard to the qualifications of individuals and possible links to political contributions. The items reproduced in this chapter illustrate both aspects of the Senate approach.

There have been cases when the Foreign Relations Committee carried its objections to the point of refusing consent, but they are extremely rare. In some instances questions were raised before the formal submission of the candidate's name, leading the administration to choose someone else. In recent times the committee has on more than one occasion admonished the executive about the quality of its ambassadorial nominees. There have been initiatives, of which one is explained in this chapter, to set standards and impose limitations by legislation.

Understanding "the view from the Senate" is thus indispensable to an appreciation of the issues involved in the choice of ambassadors. Many believe that if there is to be a change in the pattern of selection and approval, it is more likely to occur in the legislature than in the executive since every new administration comes into office burdened with the promises of a campaign and the demands of loyal followers.

The Senate itself has been the source of important research bearing on the functions and selection of ambassadors. One such study, for the Foreign Relations Committee, is featured in the introductory chapter. In this chapter we present, first, extracts from the findings of the **Jackson Committee** (Subcommittee on National Security Staffing and Operations of the Committee on Government Operations) entitled *The American Ambassador*. Published in 1964, the study was part of a series of impressive reports on various aspects of the administration of programs involving the security of the nation. Next is the article "Maxwell Gluck and All That" by **Martin F. Herz,** a retired Foreign Service officer and former ambassador to Bulgaria, who is Director of Studies of the Institute for the Study of Diplomacy and editor of this monograph. The article, abbreviated here, originally appeared in the *Foreign Service Journal* in May 1978.

The findings in 1974 of the **Watergate Committee** (Select Committee on Presidential Campaign Activities), under the heading of "Ambassadors," included a list of 31 appointees of the Nixon administration who had made financial contributions to the presidential campaign, nine of them in amounts over $100,000 (the list is not reproduced here). The Watergate Committee was able to establish a direct connection between contribution and appointment in only three cases, one of which became moot when the transaction was canceled in view of the impending investigation. (It should perhaps be noted here that since passage of the 1976 Amendments to the Federal Election Campaign Act of 1971, such large individual contributions to the campaigns of individual candidates have become illegal.) Republican Senator **Charles McC. Mathias** of Maryland explains in an article in the April 1982 *Foreign Service Journal* his proposal to set certain legislative limits to ambassadorial appointments. Finally, we reproduce the letter that **Common Cause,** the civic organization, addressed to all members of the Committee on Foreign Relations in 1977.

We express appreciation to the *Foreign Service Journal* for permission to reproduce, in condensed form, the two items that originally appeared in its pages.

The American Ambassador

Findings of the Jackson Committee

I. The Ambassador's Problem

I am sorry to know nothing more of the subject than that letter after letter has been written to you thereon, and that the office is in possession of nothing more than acknowledgements of your receipt of some of them so long ago as Aug. 1786, and still to add that your letter of Jan. 24, 1791, is the only one received of later date than May 6, 1789. You certainly will not wonder if the receipt of but one letter in two years & an half inspires a considerable degree of impatience.

Secretary of State Thomas Jefferson, Letter to William Carmichael, American Chargé in Spain, Nov. 6, 1791

Secretary Jefferson's "impatience" with Mr. Carmichael is not likely to be echoed in 1964. Today the daily volume of telegraphic traffic alone between the State Department and the embassies is more than 400,000 words.

The jet plane and electronic communications, on the one hand, and America's world involvements, on the other, have combined to complicate enormously and in part transform the role of American Ambassador.

The traditional functions—negotiation, representation, and reporting—have changed because issues can be referred rapidly to Washington, or handled by officers coming from Washington, or decided in Washington in talks with visiting heads of state, prime ministers, foreign ministers, or other high officials. If all roads once led to Rome, all airways now lead to Washington.

With respect to negotiation, the role of the modern Ambassador is much reduced—often he is but one part of a negotiating team in a complex diplomatic operation. If an issue is of some importance, the matter will probably be handled directly between the Department of State and the Foreign Office, with the Ambassador playing an intermediary or supporting role. When the Ambassador conducts negotiations, he will receive detailed instructions. To be sure, the

From *Administration of National Security: The American Ambassador,* a study submitted by the Subcommittee on National Security Staffing and Operations to the Committee on Government Operations, United States Senate (Washington, DC: U.S. Government Printing Office, 1964), pp. 1–4, 14–16.

modern Ambassador is not a mere onlooker—his advice will be sought. Particularly men in remote posts, off diplomacy's beaten tracks, or assigned to countries not at the top level of Washington concern, have some scope in practicing the art of negotiation. Even so the cables run hot and heavy, and it is a far cry from the day when an Ambassador had to operate alone for long periods, guided by his own wisdom and wit, with very general instructions.

With respect to representation, it used to be that an Ambassador represented his sovereign at the court of the other sovereign. Now things are different. An Ambassador still has the tedious round of official parties and entertainment. He must still participate in the pomp and ceremony of official life. But he must also hold the hands of newsmen, open doors for businessmen, and attend to visiting Congressmen. Besides, today's Ambassador is expected to get away from the capital and to acquire first-hand knowledge of the country's political, social and economic life. What the people are saying is often more important than the gossip of high society, and his business suits and even more informal attire may wear out sooner than his white tie and tails.

Posts, of course, vary greatly. In an emerging nation, the host government may turn to the American Ambassador for advice on economics, or administration, or military affairs, or even internal political matters which would seldom, if ever, be sought by older and more established governments. In some areas, work with regional and international organizations is an added dimension for American diplomacy.

With respect to reporting, 50 years ago it may have been sufficient to cover the affairs of the court and the capital. No more. Now an Ambassador is called upon to view the society as a whole, to analyze the forces working for change, and to relate the problems of his country to wider problems and policies. Hence his reports must penetrate more deeply while the horizon of relevance has widened—and at the same time the number of reporters other than the Ambassador has grown with the number of agencies making up the American establishment.

Thus each of the elements of an Ambassador's traditional responsibility has altered. Meanwhile, a new executive role has been laid upon our Ambassadors. Since World War II the American Executive Branch has reproduced itself abroad in something approaching its full panoply of separate agencies—with all that implies in terms of overlapping jurisdictions, incompatible assignments, mutual jealousies, surplus staff, and the ruminations of innumerable committees. Not only State, but AID, USIS, the service attachés (Army, Navy, and Air Force), military assistance advisory groups (MAAGS), CIA, Treasury, Agriculture, science attachés, and the Peace Corps may be found at our major posts. There may also be an area military commander.

In Britain, for example, with which we have old ties and many common interests, at least 44 American agencies are represented in the Embassy. In the Soviet Union, where the "court" is still a dominating fact of life, the American mission more nearly resembles the classic embassy with limited tasks. In Korea our involvement is recent but very deep and the American establishment includes sizable American forces and military bases as well as a host of civilian agencies.

Except for the Communist bloc and a few small posts where our responsibilities are limited, the number of agencies and operating programs demands on-the-spot coordination and central supervision, lest interagency pulling and hauling dissipate American influence.

To meet this need Washington has turned to the Ambassador, whose authority is reinforced by his Presidential appointment and diplomatic precedence. Gradually, if unevenly, since World War II, the Truman, Eisenhower, and especially the Kennedy Administrations have tried to build the Ambassador's coordinating role into our tradition and get it accepted in the day-to-day operations of government agencies.

But Washington giveth and Washington taketh away. In theory, the Ambassador is now more than *primus inter pares*. He is the active leader and director of American policies and programs. But practice often falls short, not least because Washington frequently undercuts the leadership and direction it asks him to provide.

In principle, our modern Chiefs of Mission are, like the President they serve, chief executives of large complex establishments, and as their other roles have changed—sometimes diminishing—this new executive role has come to the fore.

The result may be called the Ambassador's dilemma.

One: He is expected to perform his traditional diplomatic functions in a most untraditional setting, with less independence and less policy authority than Ambassadors once exercised—and with far more people under foot;

Two: He is expected to contribute to the policy process from the perspective of a single-country mission, while those at home who have to make the policies treat almost nothing as a single-country problem;

Three: He is expected to serve as leader and coordinator of his "country team" while lacking power or even much influence over the budgets, the personnel systems, the reporting requirements, and the operating policies of many of the field staffs theoretically subordinate to him.

His dilemma places a great burden on an Ambassador and ways must be found to improve and increase the support Washington gives him.

II. The President and the Ambassador

I have made choice of [John Doe], a distinguished citizen of the United States, to reside near the Government of Your Excellency in the quality of Ambassador Extraordinary and Plenipotentiary of the United States of America. He is well informed of the relative interests of the two countries and of the sincere desire of this Government to cultivate to the fullest extent the friendship which has so long subsisted between them. My knowledge of his high character and ability gives me entire confidence that he will constantly endeavor to advance the interests and prosperity of both Governments and so render himself acceptable to Your Excellency.

President Lyndon B. Johnson, Letter of Credence
of an Ambassador to a Chief of State, 1964

An Ambassador is the personal representative of our Chief of State and Government to the Chief of State to whom he is accredited.

In fact, however, most Ambassadors have only a remote relation to a President himself and are not recognized as members of his intimate official family. The very multitude of Ambassadors is one of the problems. Since 1960 the number of Chiefs of Mission to other governments has burgeoned over the one hundred mark, and this is too many for any President to know well.

A Chief of Mission customarily works in the framework of the State Department; he reports to the Department; his salary and administrative support come from the Department. The source of his instructions is normally the Secretary of State, acting for the President, or, in appropriate cases, an Assistant Secretary of State, acting for the Secretary. This is as it should be.

But, in practice, an Ambassador needs status as the President's man. Present and former Ambassadors emphasized in testimony to the Subcommittee that a chief asset an Ambassador can bring to his job is the reputation for having the special confidence and trust of the President. When an Ambassador overseas negotiates, or speaks in private or in public, his audience needs to feel that he has the confidence and speaks with the authority of the President of the United States.

"The old argument about the merits of career vs. noncareer appointments is getting a hollow ring. At present and in future most American ambassadors will come from the career Foreign Service, although there will continue to be room for noncareer ambassadors with special qualifications. There is no justification for the appointment of noncareer men and women who lack such qualifications, for there are no 'safe' posts left in today's world."

It is to the advantage of a President himself to have direct knowledge of his Chiefs of Mission. Under Secretary of State Averell Harriman made this comment to the Subcommittee:

> The more Ambassadors that the President knows personally and has confidence in, the easier it is for him to act on the advice which comes from that embassy.

More Presidential directives stating that the Ambassador is the personal representative of the President are not likely to help. Whatever can be done in this regard by Presidential letter or order has already been accomplished by the successive efforts of the last three Presidents.

It is an advantage, of course, when a President has known some of his appointees at an earlier time. But no President is likely to be widely acquainted with members of the Foreign Service, especially with those at the deputy chief of mission (DCM) level who ought to be the main source of candidates. In these circumstances, the Department of State should make a special effort to bring promising career candidates to the personal attention of a President.

Fortunately, in our time, good men do not lack occasions to

distinguish themselves, to become known to a President, and to win his respect.

Beyond that, the Department of State, the White House, and an ambassadorial appointee should cooperate to make the relationship of President and Ambassador more than routine. Hopefully, a President will come to know his key Chiefs of Mission at least as well as he does his top Washington officials and chief military leaders.

....

VI. The Ambassador in the Nation's Service

> As the personal representative of the President of the United States . . . you are part of a memorable tradition which began with Benjamin Franklin and Thomas Jefferson, and which has included many of our most distinguished citizens.
>
> President John F. Kennedy, Letter to American Ambassadors, May 29, 1961*

There is, of course, no ideal Chief of Mission. In the modern circumstances, there is heavy emphasis on the Ambassador as Executive. Strong executive leadership is important. But perhaps the most valuable attributes an Ambassador can possess are the capacity to understand the forces building up in a society and the skill to influence events in some degree in accordance with our national policy.

Today, the caliber of our Chiefs of Mission is high. The American people should be thankful for the ability and dedication of those who now head our missions abroad. But there is still room for improvement in matching persons and posts, and in keeping a competent Ambassador on the job long enough for him to become fully effective—and longer.

CAREER AND NONCAREER AMBASSADORS

In appointing an Ambassador, there is no good alternative to reliance upon the Secretary of State—working with the Director General of the Foreign Service and other top Department officers—to give the President a short slate of candidates for his consideration and choice of a nominee for proposal to the Senate for "advice and consent."

---

*[Reproduced in full in Chapter 9 below, pp. 182–84.—Ed.]

Time was when an ambassadorial post was a normal means of rewarding men for their services or contributions to a political party. It has almost passed. Today two out of three Ambassadors have risen through the ranks of the career service, and a substantial proportion of the rest qualify as professionals by virtue of long diplomatic service or experience in closely related fields.

The old argument about the merits of career versus noncareer appointments is getting a hollow ring. At present and in future most American Ambassadors will come from the career Foreign Service, although there will continue to be room for noncareer Ambassadors with special qualifications. There is no justification for the appointment of noncareer men and women who lack such qualifications, for there are no "safe" posts left in today's world.

In this matter, the occasional exception will prove the rule, and the rule is to choose an individual of unquestioned competence for the particular post.

All Embassy posts should be open to the ambition of a professional officer. In this connection Ambassador [David K. E.] Bruce commented:

> . . . to have it known that the American Government does not make it possible for a career officer, unless he has outside resources, to be Ambassador to Great Britain, I think, is almost a national shame.

Funds should be provided and allocated for maintenance allowances, entertainment, salary, etc. so that no Ambassador need draw on private means to meet the legitimate financial burdens of his post. Again, Congress take note.

If career appointees are to constitute a substantial proportion of our Chiefs of Mission, the Foreign Service must produce more senior officers of great ability. One important approach is to give promising officers throughout their career roughly a 50–50 division of service between Washington and the field, thus exposing them regularly to the wider perspectives of American government at home. Other useful steps include: the recent emphasis on more rapid promotion of outstanding younger officers; giving potential Chiefs of Mission consular posts and managerial jobs in operating agencies like AID and USIA—to test their mettle as executives; and reserving the post of deputy chief of mission to potential candidates for ambassadorial assignment. Ambassador Samuel D. Berger made this point to the Subcommittee:

The deputy position is the final testing and training ground for Ambassadors, and this assignment should be reserved for officers whose record clearly indicates that they are promising material for ambassadorships. The deputy chief of mission position should not be filled by any officer who is clearly not promising in this respect, nor should it be offered as a reward to an officer for long service, when it is clear that he cannot make the grade to Ambassador.

TOURS OF DUTY

Experience is a priceless asset, yet it is constantly thrown away by the government's traditional here-today-gone-tomorrow attitude toward Ambassadors.

We do not yet make good use of retired Ambassadors who possess particular competence in problems and areas of emerging importance. The government has only begun to tap this special reservoir of skills and experience.

The talents of our active Ambassadors are wasted by unduly abbreviated tours. The average tour of duty of Chiefs of Mission is now about 2 years and 10 months—but the shakedown period eats up about a year. In Ambassador [Livingston] Merchant's words:

> One usually has to be at a post at least a year before one has gotten one's bearings, and established one's relationships, and sensed the important people that you want to cultivate and develop, and established your own rating system for the validity of the information and the soundness of the judgments that you extract, and learned the country and its problems.

Testimony to the Subcommittee was unanimous that the average ambassadorial term abroad should be longer—except in hardship posts. . . .

A further point: The government should move fast to fill an ambassadorship that becomes vacant. And, above all, the departure of an incumbent should not be announced until the last possible moment, and should be accompanied by the designation of his successor. An Ambassador loses influence from the moment it becomes known that he is leaving—and the longer the gap between then and the arrival of his successor, the more we invite trouble in a world where trouble always seems to be waiting on the doorstep.

Maxwell Gluck and All That

Martin F. Herz

On July 2, 1957 the Committee on Foreign Relations of the United States Senate addressed the nomination of Maxwell H. Gluck, of Kentucky, to be Ambassador of the United States to Ceylon. Senator Theodore Francis Green of Rhode Island was in the chair. Senators Fulbright, Wiley and Smith attended. Senators Aiken and Capehart had given proxies to Senator Wiley.

Maxwell Gluck, whose nomination became symbolic at the time for the misuse of ambassadorial appointments as payoffs for campaign contributions, had been nominated by President Eisenhower. The nomination had the support of Senators Javits and Ives of New York and of Senators Morton and Cooper of Kentucky. According to the Washington *Post* of August 1, 1957, the Louisville *Courier-Journal* had reported Morton as saying that Javits, whose brother was a business partner of Gluck, had asked him to approve Gluck as a Kentuckian even though his residence was in New York, since he owned a horse farm near Lexington. Morton, according to that press report, said that "Javits told him New York has so many appointments it would help to have Gluck listed as from Kentucky."

Mr. Gluck had high credentials as a businessman, being the head of the Darling women's apparel chain stores, an enterprise that he had built up during 26 years until it had some 140 stores in the United States. He was also an acknowledged success as a breeder of fine horses. What troubled one member of the Senate committee, and eventually led the committee to question the Secretary of State about ambassadorial appointments, was that Mr. Gluck had no experience in international affairs, had made substantial (by the standards of 1957) financial contributions to Republican candidates, and displayed an embarrassing ignorance not only about Ceylon but also about India at his nomination hearings.

The hearing began with some desultory questioning by the Chairman. Had Mr. Gluck ever been to Ceylon? Never, but he had been "all over Europe." Did he speak any foreign language? "Some German—a little, not very much any more. I did at one time."

Reprinted by permission from the *Foreign Service Journal*, May 1978.

Senator Wiley inquired about Mr. Gluck's business experience. Senator Smith asked if his breeding of race horses took place in Kentucky, to which Mr. Gluck replied in the affirmative. The Chairman then called on Senator Fulbright, and the following colloquy ensued, according to the official record of the hearings:

SENATOR FULBRIGHT. How much did you contribute to the Republican Party in the 1956 election?

MR. GLUCK. Well, I wouldn't know offhand, but I made a contribution.

SENATOR FULBRIGHT. Well, how much?

MR. GLUCK. Let's see; I would say, all in all, twenty or thirty thousand dollars. . .

SENATOR FULBRIGHT. How much did you contribute in 1952?

MR. GLUCK. Well, not as much. I would not remember, but a fair amount.

SENATOR FULBRIGHT. Well, you are a businessman, you pay attention to your money. . .

MR. GLUCK. Yes.

SENATOR FULBRIGHT. You can guess now about how much.

MR. GLUCK. I would say around $10,000.

SENATOR FULBRIGHT. If you contributed $30,000, don't you think Ceylon is a rather remote post for that? The one who went to Belgium only contributed $11,000.

MR. GLUCK. I don't know about that, but I don't think that is the only reason.

SENATOR FULBRIGHT. You don't think that is a pertinent reason for the appointment?

MR. GLUCK. I don't think it is the only reason.

SENATOR FULBRIGHT. It is the principal reason; is it not?

MR. GLUCK. I don't think I want to admit that is the principal reason. . .

SENATOR FULBRIGHT. Why are you interested in Ceylon?

MR. GLUCK. I am not particularly interested only in Ceylon, but I am interested in a Government post where I can do some work and do some good at it. . .

SENATOR FULBRIGHT. What are the problems in Ceylon you think you can deal with?

MR. GLUCK. One of the problems are the people there, not necessarily a problem, but the relationship of the United States with the people in Ceylon. I believe I can—I think I can establish, unless we—again, unless I run into something that I have not run into before—a good relationship and good feeling toward the United States.

SENATOR FULBRIGHT. Are they not friendly with us now?

MR. GLUCK. Well, I think they are both. I think they are a people who are friendly and unfriendly, and I may be able to— . . .

SENATOR FULBRIGHT. Have you followed our relations in the Far East very closely?

MR. GLUCK. Well, just generally.

SENATOR FULBRIGHT. Do you consider we are on friendly relations with India?

MR. GLUCK. Well, I think it is more—I think a lot depends on who is there, and what they do. I don't think we are on the friendliest relations with them, but I believe it can be straightened a little more in one direction, or a little more in another direction, depending on what is done in that country.

SENATOR FULBRIGHT. Do you know our Ambassador to India?

MR. GLUCK. I know John Sherman Cooper, the previous Ambassador.

SENATOR FULBRIGHT. Did you support him in his race?

MR. GLUCK. Yes, I did.

SENATOR FULBRIGHT. And you do not know our present Ambassador?

MR. GLUCK. No, I do not . . .

SENATOR FULBRIGHT. Do you know who the Prime Minister in India is?

MR. GLUCK. Yes, but I can't pronounce his name.

SENATOR FULBRIGHT. Do you know who the Prime Minister to [sic] Ceylon is?

MR. GLUCK. I have a list—

SENATOR FULBRIGHT. Who is it?

MR. GLUCK. His name is a bit unfamiliar now. I cannot call it off, but I have obtained from Ambassador Crowe a list of all the important people there, and I went over them with him.

I have a synopsis of all the people, both Americans, ambassadors, and officials from other countries, and I have from him also a sort of little biography or history of them, with what his opinion of them is; and so—

SENATOR FULBRIGHT. That's all, Mr. Chairman.

Senator Smith then questioned Mr. Gluck about a possible

conflict of interest between his ambassadorship to Ceylon and his position on the board of directors of the World Development Corporation, and was assured there was no such conflict. The witness was then excused, and the following discussion ensued within the committee.

Senator Fulbright said Mr. Gluck "is a nice man in his business, but I think wholly unsuited to this or any other post. I don't want to raise any cain about it. We have had this up before. You [Chairman Green] wrote a letter about it. I don't think I can vote for him. I don't think we should pick him out, but I think it is ridiculous to send a man with so little preparation to an area where these people are a sensitive and strange people, and I think it will do us no good."

Senator Wiley said he started out with the presumption that when the nominee comes from the Executive, "there is back of that nomination a satisfactory conclusion; at least, that he is a man of character and ability and so forth." He also said that Senator Javits had seen him about the nomination the previous day and had praised Gluck's ability. Senator Wiley concluded that Mr. Gluck "has created a big business and done well. Therefore, I move he be reported favorably to the calendar."

Senator Wiley then added: "Now, I have lived through a number of years when the Democratic President nominated folks that had made contributions. I didn't think that disqualified them. I thought it kind of qualified them, because it showed they had an interest in their party and an interest in their Government; so that—I move he be reported favorably."

Senator Smith said he has seen Mr. Gluck the day before. "I had never met him before, but I saw him at the request of Senator Cooper and Senator Javits; and, after talking to him at some length, I felt prepared to go along with his nomination, although I was somewhat troubled that he knew nothing about the area." Then the Senator added: "That may not necessarily be a liability. It may be that a man going in there with a fresh outlook can accomplish quite a bit. He is a man familiar with business, and one who can size up things from scratch, and he may be a very valuable man." Senator Smith was prepared to second Senator Wiley's motion.

Senator Fulbright said he had not meant to leave the impression that the Democrats did not do the same thing. "I still think it is a bad practice," he said, "and I can only say that I have often voted against the Democratic nominees, too, back in those days. I think this one is unusually innocent of any knowledge of not only the area, he has not the vaguest idea who is the Prime Minister of Ceylon, India, or anything about it."

Chairman Green broke in to say: "India, he said he had—"

Senator Fulbright replied: "He could not pronounce his name. I did not want to embarrass him by asking him to spell it, but, anyway, I am not going to make a big fight about it. I am simply saying that—following up the chairman's letter, I think the Department ought to be a little more concerned about sending—especially to India and that area, Ceylon—a man with no qualifications. That ought to be a position there for a professional man. I will grant that sending a man like that to Belgium can't do much harm, because the Belgians know us, and can overlook those things. I don't think the Ceylonese or Indians will overlook a man who is totally unaware of things that are important to our relations with them."

Senator Wiley said, "You never can tell how far a frog can jump until he jumps."

To which Senator Fulbright replied, "I don't have anything special for [sic] him, but I cannot vote for him; and I must express my disapproval of this kind of appointment. I would like to ask the Chairman to remind the Department of State that he wrote them a letter about this subject not too long ago. I think it is material, in the face of our letter, that they continue to do this. I don't know what to do about it, to stop it; and I hope we stop it, whether it be a Republican or a Democrat."

There then was a vote, in which Senators Wiley and Smith voted "aye" and Senator Fulbright "no." The Chairman stated "He is confirmed," and Senator Wiley noted that he had proxies of Senators Aiken and Capehart.

It was some time before the news of this hearing hit the press, but when it did there was quite an uproar. The Washington *Post* was the first to print what it called Mr. Gluck's "closed door" testimony before the committee. In those days, however, the record of most such hearings was eventually printed and released to the public, so the Washington *Post* only advanced the time when the scandal would have become public.

Under the headline "Appointment Stirs Ceylon," the New York *Times* on August 2 reported from Colombo that "Newspapers have carried scathing comment on Mr. Gluck's apparent ignorance of Ceylonese affairs while right-wing politicians expressed disappointment about the nomination. They hold that from Mr. Gluck's performance before the Senate committee he would be no match for the envoys from the Soviet Union or Communist China.''

At the same time, the special report to the *Times* said that to Prime Minister Bandaranaike "the Ambassador-designate's remarks before the committee appear to be amusing rather than a subject for serious comment. . . . The Ceylon *Daily News,* the leading English-language newspaper here, said Mr. Gluck's replies before the Senators 'reveal a really astonishing state of affairs.' It continued: 'The only factor that appears to have influenced the selection of the new ambassador are his contributions to Republican party funds in 1952 and 1956 Presidential elections.' ''

President Eisenhower, according to a report by Chalmers Roberts in the Washington *Post* of August 1, 1957, "said with a flash of anger yesterday that he would never consider appointing anyone recommended on the basis of a political contribution." The report was headlined "Cash-Down Ambassador Hint Stirs Ike's Anger,'' and its key passages were as follows:

"He then was asked: 'In reference to another nomination, sir, were you aware when you nominated Mr. Gluck to be Ambassador to Ceylon of either the extent of his contribution to the Republican Party or his now recorded ignorance of affairs in that part of the world?' The President, visibly angry, replied that in the first place, if anybody is ever recommended to me on the basis of any contribution he has ever made to any political party, that man will never be considered. I never heard it mentioned to me as a consideration and I don't take it very kindly as suggesting I could be influenced by such things.' ''

The President gave no evidence that he thought any *particular* qualifications for appointment to ambassadorial positions were desirable or had been considered in the recommendations that he had received. The paper also reported that on the same day, August 1, the Senate Foreign Relations Committee was going to question Secretary of State Herter "behind closed doors" on State's policy in selecting ambassadors.

"Herter Defends Naming of Gluck" was the headline the following day in the New York *Times.* A story written by Russell Baker recalled the embarrassing moments of Mr. Gluck's testimony and noted, by way of introduction, that his "confession of ignorance, coupled with the admission that he had contributed between $20,000 and $30,000 to the Republican party, stirred the Foreign Relations Committee to call Mr. Herter for a discussion of political patronage and diplomatic assignments.

"Mr. Herter, armed with papers to argue that there has been no significant increase in political appointments to diplomatic posts, was with the committee in secret session for two and a half hours," the paper reported. "He supported the Gluck appointment and afterwards told newsmen that he was 'still convinced he could make a good ambassador' although the publicity had been 'unfortunate.'

"The burden of Mr. Herter's argument, however, was that so far as he knew, political financial contributions played no significant role in the selection of ambassadors. The question whether campaign contributions are an important factor behind such appointments is the central issue under debate at the Capitol, the State Department and the White House."

Mr. Herter, according to the New York *Times* story, told reporters that he had "never heard the question of contributions to any political party or individual" mentioned as a factor behind any appointment. This was substantially what President Eisenhower had said the previous day, but it still begged the question whether others, whose recommendations had led to the nomination of Mr. Gluck and similarly unqualified candidates for ambassadorial positions, might not have been motivated more directly by financial contributions made to the party.

The Gluck appointment, the story noted, was the third diplomatic appointment to stir controversy that year. The others had been the nomination of Scott McLeod as Ambassador to Ireland and Henry J. Taylor as Ambassador to Switzerland. (Mr. McLeod had been Senator Joseph McCarthy's hatchet man in the State Department. Mr. Taylor had written a favorable biography of President Eisenhower.) The New York *Times* noted that both candidates had been found to be "innocent of diplomatic experience" and that Mr. Taylor had been questioned by the Foreign Relations Committee "about his professions of belief in the existence of flying saucers."

The Chairman of the Senate Foreign Relations Committee, according to press reports on August 2, seemed to have a change of mind about the qualifications of Maxwell Gluck. He was reported as declaring that he thought Mr. Gluck "should not have been appointed. He doesn't have the qualifications." The New York *Times* noted that the hearings on Mr. Gluck's nomination had been held in secret by Senator Green's Committee and that after its favorable report the full Senate had approved it without objection. It is noteworthy that while Senator Green *after* the hearings mentioned the aspect of qualifications for senior diplomatic appointments, neither President Eisenhower nor Secretary of State Herter addressed that aspect, confining themselves to denials that money considerations had played a role in the appointment process as far as they themselves were concerned. . . .

In an editorial on August 1, 1957, the New York *Times* took the position that while the hearings had disclosed that Mr. Gluck "knew little or nothing about Ceylon and South Asia, this does not prove that Mr. Gluck will turn out to be a bad Ambassador to Ceylon. He may be very good. That depends on his ability, intelligence, attractiveness and the amount of work he does."

Having thus apparently conceded that prior acquaintance with international affairs might be irrelevant to the performance of an ambassador to a country whose customs, mores, traditions and political institutions differed significantly from those of the United States, the editorial rectified that impression by adding: "However, it is clear that the White House has chosen someone without any previous qualifications for that particular post . . ." It then remarked, somewhat lamely: "The United States diplomatic service does not have enough career officers of ambassadorial rank to go around. In any event we have always used private citizens as envoys." And the editorial went on to cite some brilliant examples of non-career ambassadors such as Ellsworth Bunker, who had served with distinction in Argentina and Italy before going to India, and David K. E. Bruce, who had done outstanding work in Paris and was then in Bonn. The editorial concluded: "There seems to be no rule to follow. It is up to the White House and State Department to pick qualified men. They do not always do so."

The editorial's statement that the Foreign Service did not "have enough career officers of ambassadorial rank to go around" did not go unchallenged. In a Letter to the Editor, Ambassador Robert McClintock, writing on behalf of the editorial board of the *Foreign Service Journal,* gave a diplomatically soft but rather telling response:

'It has been our impression," the McClintock letter said, "that the American Foreign Service, with the high standards it has maintained over the years, does in fact produce career officers who merit ambassadorial rank. That this impression is shared by the President, the Secretary of State, and the Senate seems borne out by the fact that 53 chiefs-of-mission posts are held by career officers as compared with 23 not of the career. So far as we are aware, there is, furthermore, no dearth of other career officers whose qualifications and experience qualify them for ambassadorial rank.''

The letter also rejected the idea that certain posts had to be reserved for rich men because of the inadequate pay that career officers received. If this was the problem, the letter said, ''we believe that a great majority of the American people would support Congress in paying all Ambassadors adequate representation and other allowances . . .'' And with ambassadorial tongue in cheek McClintock concluded: ''We likewise believe that the great majority of the American people support the President in his statement on not granting ambassadorial posts on the basis of campaign contributions.''

Ambassadorships

Findings of the Watergate Committee

In a February 25, 1974, news conference, President Nixon denied that his administration was involved in the practice of brokering ambassadorships. He declared, "Ambassadorships have not been for sale and I would not approve an ambassadorship unless the man or woman was qualified clearly apart from his contribution." That very day, his personal attorney and one of his principal fundraisers. Herbert Kalmbach, became the first person in recent times to be convicted for "selling an ambassadorship," in violation of title 18, United States Code, section 600. On February 25, 1974, Mr. Kalmbach entered a guilty plea to having promised, in 1971, then Ambassador to Trinidad and Tobago, J. Fife Symington, a more prestigious European ambassadorship in return for a $100,000 contribution, which was to be split between 1970 Republican senatorial candidates designated by the White House and Mr. Nixon's 1972 campaign. A condition of Mr. Kalmbach's agreement to plead guilty was that he be granted immunity from further prosecution in connection with "contributions from persons seeking ambassadorial posts." Mr. Kalmbach has also advised the committee staff that then Ambassador to Jamaica, Vincent de Roulet, had a similar commitment.

Since his reelection on November 7, 1972, Mr. Nixon apparently has had little trouble finding large contributors who were "qualified apart from their contributions" to be appointed as Ambassadors. Since November 7, 1972, Mr. Nixon has appointed 13 noncareer Ambassadors. Eight of these newly appointed and confirmed Ambassadors each had donated a minimum of $25,000 and in the aggregate, they contributed over $706,000 to their appointer's reelection committee.

In fact, over $1.8 million in Presidential campaign contributions can be attributed in whole, or in part, to persons holding ambassadorial appointments from the the President. . . .

Excerpts from *The Final Report of the Select Committee on Presidential Campaign Activities,* United States Senate, pursuant to S. Res. 60, Feb. 7, 1973, a Resolution to Establish a Select Committee of the Senate to Investigate and Study Illegal or Improper Campaign Activities in the Presidential Election of 1972 (Washington, DC: U.S. Government Printing Office, June 1974), pp. 492–496.

Furthermore, the committee's investigation indicates there are still a number of large contributors whose ambassadorial aspirations are yet unfulfilled. Six large contributors, who gave an aggregate of over $3 million, appear to have been actively seeking appointments at the time of their contributions.

At present, 34 of 112, or about 30 percent of all foreign envoy posts abroad are held by noncareer appointees. The largest concentration of noncareer ambassadors is in Western Europe, where there is also a high concentration of persons contributing $100,000 or over. . . .

Senator Claiborne Pell, a member of the Senate Foreign Relations Committee, said of the Belgium, Netherlands, and Luxembourg appointments:

> And in this regard we ought to bear in mind that Benelux seems to be the most expensive place on which to be appointed because Mrs. Farkas, who is Ambassador to Luxembourg, and she wasn't appointed until her contribution had been put to the barrelhead even though an agreement had been received 6 or 8 months earlier, contributed $300,000; Mr. Gould, who was not very forthcoming in his testimony as far as his wife's contribution went, less than candid, as I said publicly at the time, contributed $100,000; and Mr. Firestone will have contributed $168,000; so it means that . . . the Ambassador[s] to Benelux will have contributed over a half-million dollars, substantially over a half-million dollars, and I think it is a poor practice.

The Caribbean posts of Jamaica and Trinidad-Tobago were also popular with Presidential contributors. Sumner Gerard, appointed to the Jamaican post in February 1974, gave $38,867, while Lloyd Miller, Ambassador to Trinidad and Tobago since December 1973, donated $25,000. The two former envoys to these posts, Vincent de Roulet and J. Fife Symington, each contributed $100,000, allegedly as part of an effort to obtain appointments to more pestigious ambassadorial posts.

According to the FCRP[1] fundraisers interviewed by the Select Committee, they went to great pains to tell prospective contributors who might be interested in ambassadorial posts that there was no quid pro quo in exchange for any contribution they might give. Robert Gray, a public relations executive and a fundraiser in the 1972 Presidential campaign who had been recruited by Maurice Stans, had a set speech when making solicitations in this context. Speaking of his solicitation of John Safer, a Washington, D.C.,

---

[1] Finance Committee to Reelect the President.

developer and sculptor who gave $250,000 to the reelection campaign, Gray testified:

> [H]e did tell me that he wanted . . . to be considered for an ambassadorship. Over the years I have learned the speech almost by rote, which I gave to him as I have given every time that the subject comes up; and that is almost verbatim as I have given it that only the President can guarantee you that you can be an ambassador. No one else can guarantee that you will be nominated to the Senate other than he, and that any contribution from any citizen can do no more than assure him or guarantee that those of us who are involved in the fundraising process will do our best to see that his name is among those considered. And then he will be considered on the basis of qualifications at levels beyond ours.[2]

Gray communicated Safer's interest in making a contribution as well as his interest in Government service to Stans. Apparently, Safer was also referred to Herbert Kalmbach who reiterated that his interest in an ambassadorship would be forwarded to the proper persons, including Maurice Stans, but that no quid pro quo could follow from the contribution.

At the very least, a number of persons saw the making of a contribution as a means of obtaining the recognition needed to be actively considered. Thus . . . Vincent de Roulet stated that he saw his contributions as one of three or four avenues available to individuals to obtain an appointment. In fact, one businessman, Roy Carver, chairman of the board of Bandag, Inc., apparently saw a correlation between the size of the contribution and the extent of the anticipated recognition. Robert Gray testified that his public relations firm, Hill & Knowlton, had been retained by Carver to gain "greater visibility on the Washington scene." As related by Gray, Carver later told him that he was "anxious to be considered as an ambassador." Although Gray had given Carver his "pat speech," Carver wanted to make contributions as a means whereby he would receive "consideration"—but not necessarily the appointment. Gray described his contacts with Carver:

> MR. DORSEN. Was any discussion had between you and Mr. Carver concerning the amount of contribution?
>
> MR. GRAY. No, not at any time. [M]y understanding is that he gave a heavy contribution in the end. The only thing that I know is that during the campaign he would call every so often to find out if I could tell him what other people had given, who was top money man at the moment; because he, particularly in the final weeks, got very anxious that he be on record as having given more than someone else. I don't know if he ended up with that distinction

---

[2]Gray executive session, March 12, 1974, 8–9.

or not; but he likes to be first in what he does, and he was determined in the final weeks to be first if he could.

MR. DORSEN. Did you communicate with him the amount that you thought would give him the highest contribution of the campaign?

MR. GRAY. Yes, At times when I could have found that out I would pass it on to him.

MR. DORSEN. How did you find this out?

MR. GRAY. By calling Ms. [Arden] Chambers [Stans' secretary] usually.

* * * * *

MR. DORSEN. Did his desire to give the largest contribution in the campaign have anything to do with his desire to become an ambassador?

MR. GRAY. With his desire to be considered as an ambassador? Yes, I am sure that it did. I cannot imagine that he would have given those kinds of moneys without that belief.

MR. DORSEN. Did you and he discuss the possibility that he would give the largest contribution in the campaign, would tend to increase the amount of consideration he would get for his—

MR. GRAY. No, it was not that. The amount of visibility he would get I think is what intrigued him about the amount.

On November 2, 1972, Carver gave Bandag, Inc. stock worth approximately $257,000 to the President's campaign. Although Carver received a number of State Department and White House interviews, he never received any appointment.

In at least two cases, discussed in greater detail below, there is evidence that the articulated policy of the Finance Committee to Reelect the President not even to suggest the possibility of a *quid pro quo* to a prospective contributor was ignored by high-ranking White House and campaign officials.[3] According to evidence in the possession of the committee, in two cases, involving J. Fife Symington and Vincent de Roulet, Herbert Kalmbach, the President's personal attorney and the leading fundraiser on behalf of FCRP prior to April 7, 1972, appears to have made an express commitment for an ambassadorial post in exchange for a substantial campaign contribution. In one of these cases, involving Symington, Kalmbach has already pleaded guilty to a violation of title 18, United States Code, section 600, which makes it a crime to offer a Government job in exchange for a political contribution. In a third case, involving

---

[3]Perhaps in no other area of the campaign financing investigation was the inability to obtain White House documents as important as was the case involving ambassadorial appointments. Since the appointment is made by the President and final consideration of the merits of a particular candidate did not extend significantly beyond the walls of the White House, the internal White House documents reviewing the qualifications of a candidate could be particularly enlightening. As noted elsewhere in this report, no documents were provided to the committee following the conclusion of public hearings on August 7, 1973.

Cornelius Vanderbilt Whitney, a $250,000 contribution was returned to Whitney in the expectation that he would have to testify before the Senate Foreign Relations Committee and that the return would eliminate any suggestion that the anticipated appointment was related to a campaign gift.[4] [The rest of this chapter of the Select Committee's report details the cases involving J. Fyfe Symington, Vincent de Roulet, and C.V. Whitney—Ed.]

---

[4]In a fourth case, involving Ruth L. Farkas, the Select Committee refrained from conducting an investigation into any relationship between her campaign contribution of $300,000 and her nomination to the post of Ambassador to Luxembourg at the request of the office of Special Prosecutor.

Compliance with this request of the office of the Special Prosecutor was one of several such actions by the committee.

Politics or Merit?

Charles McC. Mathias Jr.

To understand some of the problems about how we choose our ambassadors, it is useful to consider the unique historical experience which has shaped our attitude towards diplomacy and diplomats. When the United States won its independence, it also broke with European diplomatic practice. During the nineteenth century, while most of the countries of Europe moved toward professionalizing their diplomatic corps, the United States moved in a different direction. The newly independent republic looked upon ambassadorial rank and privilege with a jaundiced eye and found it undemocratic. It viewed European courts as nests of intrigue, and it distrusted diplomats who spent years abroad subject to foreign influences, believing they emerged tainted from the experience. As a result, the United States sent few envoys abroad and did not give even these the rank of ambassador. More importantly, the first American diplomats were consciously chosen from the mainstream of American life and, as was the case with William Pinkney, returned to other careers following their diplomatic service.

Perhaps nothing symbolizes more the uniqueness of American diplomatic practice in this period than that five of the first eight presidents (both John Adams and John Quincy Adams, Jefferson, Monroe, and Van Buren) served as American ministers resident abroad. Not only was this without parallel in Europe at the time, but, even today, it stands as unique in diplomatic history. The outstanding individuals who served the United States abroad in those early years, among them, of course, Benjamin Franklin, created a legacy which strongly reinforced the idea that a professional diplomatic corps was both unnecessary and undesirable.

Over the last two-thirds of the nineteenth century and into the early twentieth century, this legacy tended to obscure the uglier realities of the spoils system and patronage politics. Beginning with Andrew Jackson, continuing through Ulysses S. Grant and even Woodrow Wilson, chiefs of U.S. missions abroad were chosen largely from the ranks of the president's friends and supporters.

Reprinted by permission from the *Foreign Service Journal*, April 1982.

With each change in party in the White House, qualified and unqualified American ministers were packed off to be replaced by others who had earned their posts through family ties, political influence, or campaign support. General Grant sent his brother-in-law to Denmark, his secretary's uncle to Belgium, and a military crony to Spain. None distinguished himself. Woodrow Wilson's appointments were described by diplomatic historian E. Wilder Spaulding as, for the most part, "a nondescript team of lame ducks, nonentities, and political innocents."

Of course, there also were some distinguished representatives during this period. Charles Francis Adams, whom President Lincoln selected to serve as minister to London during the difficult Civil War years, proved to be a superb choice. Adams's diplomatic skill in maintaining British neutrality contributed greatly to the Union victory. But, in choosing Adams, Lincoln seems to have been motivated more by domestic political considerations than by Adams's qualifications for the post. In a biography of his father, Charles Francis Adams, Jr. compares Lincoln's approach to filling this sensitive diplomatic post with the way the president would select a local postmaster.

Over time, revelations of corruption and incompetence gradually nudged the country toward a career service based on merit. Meanwhile, a few skilled diplomats, such as Eugene Schuyler, William Scruggs, and Henry White, managed to survive the changes of administration to form the core of a professional diplomatic service. In 1924, passage of the Foreign Service Act was a major step toward creating a pool of experienced career diplomats from which ambassadorial appointments could be made. In that year, 18 of 51 chiefs of mission were career officers. By 1928, some 30 of 58 chiefs of mission were career. Throughout the remainder of the period between the two world wars, the career segment in the ambassadorial ranks remained close to the 50 percent mark.

The next jump in the percentage of career chiefs of mission came after World War II. As the United States assumed global responsibilities and the number of overseas missions expanded, the percentage of career chiefs of mission rose in an almost unbroken line to 71 percent by 1960. For the next 20 years, the percentage of career ambassadors hovered around the 70 percent mark. It dropped as low as 64 percent one year under President Kennedy and rose to a high of 78 percent one year under President Carter. Changes in campaign financing laws, increases in some representation allowances, and Congressional insistence on more qualified nominees have all helped to establish more firmly the career principle.

Nevertheless, no president in recent memory has resisted the temptations and pressures to make patronage appointments. . . .

Reviewing the record of the Reagan administration, as well as the record of the previous administration, convinces me that the time has come to end what George Kennan once called "diplomacy by dilettantism." The bill I have introduced, S. 1886, the Chiefs of Diplomatic Missions Bill, would help us do that. S. 1886 would amend the Foreign Service Act of 1980 to provide that not less than 85 percent of the total number of chiefs of mission be members of the career service.

The approach which this bill takes is not new. In 1973, Arkansas' J. William Fulbright, then-chairman of the Senate Foreign Relations Committee, tried unsuccessfully to pass legislation limiting the percentage of non-career ambassadors. In each of the next two years, I introduced bills placing a 20-percent limit on non-career appointments. Although neither of these measures passed, the Senate in 1976 did adopt my compromise amendment to the State Department authorization bill providing for a 25-percent limit on non-career ambassadors. In the conference with the House, the amendment was watered down to a mild statement of support for a "greater number" of career ambassadors.

Obviously, limiting the percentage of non-career ambassadors does not in itself ensure that qualified ambassadors will be selected. There is no way that Congress can legislate quality appointments. Nor is it my intention to exclude qualified non-career individuals from consideration as ambassadors. The concept of the non-professional ambassador is deeply rooted in our history, and many Americans who were not professional diplomats have made outstanding contributions to American diplomacy. We will continue to need the new ideas and fresh perspective which they bring to diplomacy.

My intention in introducing S. 1886 is to control the abuse of ambassadorial appointments for patronage purposes and to strengthen the career service. To achieve these objectives, the bill would affect the nomination and confirmation process in three ways:

• First, the bill if enacted into law, would encourage more careful scrutiny of non-career appointments within the administration. A president who knows that he has a limited number of non-career appointments can be expected to make choices with considerable care;

• Second, a limit on non-career ambassadors would act as a shield to protect well-intentioned administrations from the temptations and pressures of patronage politics. And it would restrain administrations more prone to spoils than to merit;

• Third, a limit on non-career appointments would offset the strong bias in the Senate in favor of confirmation of nominees.

As any long-time observer of the confirmation process knows, the Senate rarely challenges a president's ambassadorial nominations. Most members of the Senate believe the president is entitled to have those whom he wants serving him. In general, we have neither the time nor the inclination to engage in bruising battles over a single ambassadorial nomination, unless the selection is palpably egregious. Politically, there is little to be gained from such a fight, and contrary to the stereotype, most senators do not enjoy grilling a hapless nominee in front of his family and friends. It is unrealistic, then, to expect that the confirmation process will screen out any but the most obviously unqualified nominees.

My main aim in limiting the number of non-career chiefs of mission is to strengthen the career service. Obviously, there have been career ambassadors who were not qualified for their posts. Every Foreign Service officer has a favorite horror story to tell. And it would be naive to assume that all future career ambassadors will be qualified. However, in the long run, the best hope for having consistently well-qualified ambassadors clearly lies in strengthening the career service. One of the most important ways of accomplishing this is to increase the prospect that career officers can aspire to the highest positions in their profession. Without this possibility, it is difficult to see how we can continue to attract and retain trained, dedicated individuals at a time when Foreign Service life involves increasing hardships and danger. Limiting non-career appointments is not just a matter of fairness to the career service, it is a question of the best interests of the country.

Whatever the fate of S. 1886, it is obvious that the United States needs more than ever to be represented abroad by the best men and women we can find. Perhaps we cannot aspire to the heights of those glorious years when future presidents represented America abroad. But we can certainly aspire to a better system than we have now. Skillful diplomacy is more important today to the security of the United States than at any time since the Republic was created. The United States now finds itself in a world in which it cannot readily impose its will on others nor retreat to the safety of isolation. Where we once could use military or economic power to work our will in the world, we now find ourselves constrained and our options limited. The United States can no longer go it alone. As crises in Poland, Afghanistan, and the Mideast show, we need the support of our allies, we need the cooperation of non-aligned countries, and we need to communicate clearly with our potential adversaries. Bargaining, negotiation, and consensus building are the order of the day. To succeed in such a world, we must ensure that our side of the table is peopled with skilled and experienced diplomats. . . .

A Letter From Common Cause

To the Members of the Committee on Foreign Relations, United States Senate

June 1, 1977

Dear Senator:

Common Cause has become increasingly concerned that the process of confirming nominees to the post of ambassador is seriously deficient. Hearings are being held with little advance notice to the public, which undermines the ability of knowledgeable persons and organizations to contribute their views on the qualifications of the nominees.

Further, there is little of the scrutiny which is necessary in order for the Senate to carry out its Constitutionally prescribed mandate. Such confirmation hearings are superfluous rituals which, as past experience has shown, can result in a too hasty ratification of White House nominees. This lack of care perpetuates the possibility that people will be appointed ambassador who lack the necessary expertise to effectively carry out American foreign policy.

We strongly urge that the Committee establish procedures for conducting hearings on career and non-career appointees. Such procedures would insure a serious, in-depth examination of each nominee and should be in place before any new ambassadors are confirmed. We believe the public has the right to expect as much care and deliberation from the Senate in the confirmation process as it does from the President in his selections.

At a minimum, we suggest the following guidelines:

1. Notice to the general public of hearing should be made seven days in advance of the hearing date.

2. The Committee should engage in broad and extensive questioning of the nominee's expertise and should carefully investigate his or her past record.

3. Voting on the nominee should be postponed for at least two weeks after the hearings to allow time for Committee members to study the hearing record.

4. A report on each nominee should be issued to the Senate at least three full days prior to a Senate vote.

The Committee will be looking at approximately forty nominees for ambassadorial posts in the coming months. We strongly urge that procedures such as we have recommended be put in place so that the remaining nominees will be subjected to the degree of scrutiny by the Senate Foreign Relations Committee that the public has a right to expect.

Sincerely,

David Cohen
President

Common Cause
2030 M Street, N.W.
Washington, DC 20036

6

In Favor of Non-Career Appointments

The United States has throughout its history been ambivalent on the question of ambassadors. There was a time at the beginning of our republic when some asked whether the nation should appoint ambassadors at all; the title was considered an undesirable reminder of the European monarchies. Yet, as we have seen, some of the greatest of the early American statesmen served with distinction in the role of ambassador. As the country saw less need for effective diplomacy, the title and the appointments became rewards for political favors; the domestic spoils system was applied to diplomacy as well.

In the twentieth century, the picture has been mixed. Awareness of the need for professional diplomacy led to the creation of the modern Foreign Service. At the same time, presidents, never totally sure of the competence and loyalty of the professionals, have chosen envoys also from private life. Some of these have been among the greatest representatives and negotiators in our history. Others demonstrated inexperience and a lack of talent. The Senate, charged by the Constitution to "advise and consent," has to date seldom reversed a presidential choice. Ways to improve the review process have been frequently discussed, seldom tried.

Where *should* ambassadors be sought? This chapter and the two that follow present the principal arguments in the career vs. non-career debate.

* * * * *

Much of the debate that goes on over the appointment of non-career persons as ambassadors centers on the assumption that the majority of such appointments are to pay back political debts. The issue, however, goes deeper: Is not the conduct of foreign policy quintessentially political? If so, should not the top personnel entrusted with the conduct of such affairs of state be themselves political persons rather than career "bureaucrats"? Do not such "political" appointees best represent a country's prevailing political currents and philosophy?

No one has more ably argued the case for "political" appointments than **Laurence H. Silberman,** a former U.S. deputy attorney general and ambassador to Yugoslavia, in a famous article in *Foreign Affairs* in 1979, here reprinted in condensed form with permission of the publishers. While his argument deals with "policy officers" and thus mainly with political appointees in the State Department, it constitutes also a rationale for politically appointed ambassadors—and indeed he recommends that the most important embassies be headed by political appointees. In another article from the same journal, **Clare Boothe Luce,** former ambassador to Italy, makes a similar case (also condensed) though in somewhat different terms. Most recently, in discussing the proposal of Senator Mathias (see Chapter 5), the Heritage Foundation, a reputable conservative think tank, questioned virtually all the arguments for career appointments. This point of view is set out in the Foundation's issue paper by **John Krizay,** a former Foreign Service officer who is currently a professor of economics and free-lance writer.

We thank *Foreign Affairs* and the Heritage Foundation for permission to reprint.

Toward Presidential Control of the State Department

Laurence H. Silberman

This article challenges the notion that it is appropriate for Foreign Service officers to routinely occupy senior policymaking positions in the State Department. As a recent "political" ambassador who has also served at a senior level in domestic departments of our government, I confess that I ended my ambassadorial stint with less than friendly feelings toward the Foreign Service as a whole. Since then, reflecting as dispassionately as possible on my own observations and looking with some care into past history, I have concluded that the frictions that have arisen almost continuously between the Service and successive Presidents (and their political appointees) have their roots deep in the system of appointments itself—and that they lend themselves to constructive remedies. . . .

Among the world democracies, the United States uniquely functions with so many political appointments at senior levels of government. But the United States' tripartite governmental structure is also unique. The parliamentary democracies fuse legislative and executive powers; the civil service in those countries, therefore, looks only to one political authority. By contrast, in the United States both a presidential sun and a congressional moon exert a gravitational pull on the Civil Service. Since our chief executive must compete with legislative authority for the allegiance, or even the attention, of the Civil Service, it follows that he needs a considerable number of senior executives in the departments who are closely tied to his political fortunes. Even these ties do not guarantee him bureaucratic support, but they ensure an irreducible minimum of influence. . . .

The Foreign Service has persistently argued for a congressionally imposed limit on the number or percentage of non-career appointments to ambassadorships and has grumbled at what it regards as excessive appointments of non-careerists to comparable positions in Washington. A necessary corollary to the Service's position has

Excerpted from *Foreign Affairs,* Spring 1979, reprinted by permission. Copyright 1979 by the Council on Foreign Relations, Inc.

119

been its explicit assumption that foreign policy—unlike all other responsibilities of government—is not appropriately a subject for political difference. As Fred Iklé recently put it, the Foreign Service has a direct career interest in defending the cliché that "politics stops at the water's edge."[1]

George Kennan, perhaps the leading apostle of foreign policy careerism (some say elitism), argues that our political parties play no important role in the long-term formulation of foreign policy because in the United States, unlike Europe, they are not ideological. He sees them as purely pragmatic groupings of various constituencies without ideological content. When politicians challenge the Foreign Service's conduct of policy, they are, according to Kennan, responding merely to "highly organized lobbies and interest groups."[2]

The ultra-careerist must thus denigrate the impact of politics on foreign policy, for if it were conceded that our political parties do represent alternative philosophies of foreign policy, it would also have to be conceded, consistent with democratic theory, that the successful party is entitled to place its adherents in senior State Department positions to carry out its philosophy.

Kennan and his supporters, I submit, fundamentally misunderstand our political system. American political parties can indeed be seen as competitive constituency groupings, but these have always been bound together in significant degree by an ideological glue of varying viscosity—using "ideology" simply to mean a reasonably coherent set of ideas about the relationship between government and its citizens. Our great geographical and cultural diversity, as virtually every first-year college student is taught, has caused a certain degree of ideological overlapping. Still, for almost 50 years the Republican Party, or at least its central core, has differed with the Democrats over the fundamental issue of the desirability, equity, even morality of coercive redistribution of wealth and income, and the corollary question of the growth of governmental power.

Moreover—and this point is crucial—domestic ideological differences have always been, in part, reflected in the differing foreign policy approaches of the Democratic and Republican Parties. Surely

---

[1] "Beyond the Water's Edge: Responsible Partisanship in Foreign Policy," *Common Sense*, Summer 1978.

[2] "Foreign Policy and the Professional Diplomat," *Wilson Quarterly*, Winter 1977, pp. 148-57.

the restrained enthusiasm with which conservative Republicans view delegations of authority to the United Nations is ideologically connected to Republican distrust of domestic governmental growth, and the greater receptiveness with which most liberal Democrats examine the developing nations' demand for a New International Economic Order is related to their espousal of domestic economic redistribution. For most liberal Democrats, "narrowing the gap" in world income by direct transfers of wealth follows ineluctably from their domestic political objective of similarly "narrowing the income gap" among Americans. Domestic liberals—and most are Democrats—are almost as prone to believe that world order can be achieved through supranational planning as they are to believe that we should move toward greater governmental planning domestically. Conservatives, by contrast, in both domestic and foreign policy, tend to distrust rationalistic schemes and give greater deference to the natural growth of domestic and international structures. These differences, between liberal and conservative, go back to Rousseau and Burke. . . .

"Career officers typically complain that politicians and political appointees do not sufficiently appreciate 'the world as it is.' In a sense that is true. The Foreign Service will more accurately reflect trends and values prevailing outside the United States than the noncareerists. But, I believe, the converse is also true: The Service will less accurately reflect counterpart trends and values dominant within the United States."

I do not mean to suggest that American foreign policy will or should shift 180 degrees as administrations change. In the first place, the great strength of American democracy is the relatively narrow degree of ideological differences between our political parties with respect to *either* domestic or foreign issues. What we virtually all agree upon—our shared premises—is greater than that which divides us. Therefore, philosophic changes in foreign policy orientations, while significant, will not be fundamental—not sea changes. . . .

Some scholars argue that ideology should play little or no role in the conduct of foreign policy, but it is hard to take that position seriously. Can one imagine American policy in this century uninfluenced by antipathy to or a healthy fear of fascism and communism? Nonetheless, how much weight ideology should be given when fashioning policy toward other nations is surely questionable. As Bayless Manning put it, since the beginning of the Republic pragmatism and ideology, held in uneasy balance, have been twin themes of our foreign policy.[3] Sometimes an administration has emphasized ideological factors over pragmatic ones, for example, Woodrow Wilson's self-determination, John Foster Dulles' anti-communism, and Jimmy Carter's human rights. At other times, as most recently with Kissinger's Realpolitik, pragmatism seems to dominate.

I suggest that a long-term aim of our policy is to keep these considerations, ideology and pragmatism, in appropriate balance. No magic formula, however, will permanently achieve that equation. The best means to keep these factors in balance, and the one most appropriate to our system of government, is partisan public debate. Inevitably, the administration in power will emphasize one or the other factor and the party out of power will duly criticize the administration for overemphasis—just as the Democrats attacked Dulles for excessive moralizing and Kissinger for too little attention to moral concerns. The political process ensures that the balance can never be tipped too far in one direction.

In that fashion, I would argue, partisan political debate over foreign policy serves long-run stability rather than instability. The democratic process is often thought to jeopardize professionally devised foreign policy continuity; in fact, it ensures a deeper continuity which eludes totalitarian states. The key theoretical proposition, then, of the careerists' argument for their own dominance of senior foreign policy positions—that domestic politics is the appropriate process for the resolution of domestic economic and social issues, but *not* for foreign policy questions—is plainly and demonstrably wrong. . . .

The Foreign Service ambassador will often (but by no means always) have a deeper knowledge of the country to which he or she is assigned than a non-careerist, but the non-careerist often has a comparative advantage in understanding the United States, particularly if he or she comes to a post with a broad background in government, economics or scholarship.

---

[3]Bayless Manning, "Goals, Ideology and Foreign Policy," *Foreign Affairs*, January 1976, pp. 271–284.

Career officers typically complain that politicians and political appointees do not sufficiently appreciate "the world as it is." In a sense that is true. The Foreign Service will more accurately reflect trends and values prevailing outside the United States than the non-careerists. But, I believe, the converse is also true: the Service will less accurately reflect counterpart trends and values dominant within the United States. The Foreign Service in the 1920s, 1930s and 1940s was significantly more sympathetic to dominant trends in Western Europe during that time, including what we have come to see as misguided ideas of accommodation with fascism, than was the Roosevelt Administration.[4] Today, I would argue that the Foreign Service is more willing to accommodate Marxist trends around the world than are many politicians or the American people as a whole. Essentially that is why Daniel Patrick Moynihan as U.N. Ambassador was so popular with the American public but so repugnant to our professionals. . . .

The Foreign Service officer has a natural tendency toward caution; one advances in the Foreign Service by not making mistakes. It follows, then, that risk is to be avoided. One kind of avoidable risk involves too sharp a presentation of options. Just as a diplomat must often seek to paper over disputes between his own country and his assigned country, he learns to blur American foreign policy options for presentation to policymakers. Thus the State Department's nickname, "the Fudge Factory."

The other kind of risk typically eschewed by career officers is too vigorous a defense of American interests because such behavior can lead to relative unpopularity with the nation or group of nations in which the officer specializes—particularly if that group of nations shares a common ideology. For instance, two political appointees of Roosevelt in the 1930s, Claude G. Bowers to Spain and William E. Dodd to Germany, were far more outspoken in defending American values and ideology in the face of fascist attacks than the prevailing views within the career service or, in the case of Dodd, his career-service successor.[5] . . .

---

[4]See Martin Weil, *A Pretty Good Club,* New York: W.W. Norton, 1978, especially pp. 94–102 and 119–28.

[5]Both Dodd and Bowers are discussed in the anecdotal but useful gallery of ambassadorial portraits by E. Wilder Spaulding, *Ambassadors Ordinary and Extraordinary,* Washington, D.C.: Public Affairs Press, 1961, pp. 170–77. For a more considered comparison of Dodd and his successor, Hugh Wilson, see Arnold A. Offner, *American Appeasement,* Cambridge: Harvard University Press, 1969, pp. 206–16. How much of Hitler's well-known view of the

It is sometimes observed—Harold Nicolson, the British counterpart to George Kennan, said it patronizingly—that career diplomats are trained to patience, whereas amateurs often blunder by seeking to accomplish too much during their relatively short tenure. There is a good deal of truth to that, but the other side of the coin is that the Foreign Service office is often slow to see the importance of change, and "the essence of good foreign policy is constant reexamination."[6] For this reason, I believe we need both careerists and non-careerists among our diplomats. . . .

The career Foreign Service officer will, and indeed should, exercise a cautious drag on political swings in foreign policy direction. Any government bureaucracy will do the same, since it has an intellectual and psychological investment in past policy. Particularly is this important in foreign affairs, since other nations, too, have investments in these policies. Capricious turns of the foreign policy wheel will inevitably undermine U.S. credibility. But the Foreign Service's challenge to the *legitimacy* of senior political appointees in the State Department does not serve a policy interest because it does not actually focus on policy. More, it extends beyond advice regarding fashioning of policy to constitute obstruction of the implementation of policy. And this, in a vicious circle, tends to generate within political authority a disposition to disregard completely whatever the Foreign Service has to contribute. . . .

Three competing interests, then, are involved here. First, democratic control of foreign policy requires political presidential appointments in the State Department just as is the case with all other government departments. Second, the debilitating friction between administrations and the Foreign Service must be reduced. Third, spokesmen for the Foreign Service are right to concern us all with maintaining the morale of the Service. If a career officer cannot look forward to the day he or she is appointed an ambassador, we will not continue to attract top-grade talent into the Foreign Service. That consideration has led Service spokesmen to urge Congress to limit by statute the number or percentage of non-career ambassadorial appointments. The Constitution, in my view, however, will not tolerate such legislative limitations on the presidential appointment power.

---

weakness of Western democracies arose from his perception of Western professional diplomats?

[6] David Halberstam, *The Best and The Brightest*, New York: Random House, 1972, p. 121.

These three conflicting policy interests—to encourage political control, to reduce competitive friction and to ensure a fixed percentage of ambassadorships for Foreign Service officers—can be accommodated. I propose a law that would convert all but a set number of ambassadorships, say 15 or 20, into appointments of the Secretary of State.[7] Incumbents would be limited to career officers and would carry their Foreign Service grade (normally at the top or close to it), but *not* an executive-level rank commensurate with senior presidential appointments. Of course, this would change the ostensible nature of these ambassadorships; they would no longer be seen as policymaking positions. But the truth of the matter is that few ambassadorships today are in practice real policymaking positions. As has been remarked too often, advances in transportation and communications have erased much discretion that ambassadors were once called upon to exercise. For the same reason, it is more a fiction than fact to describe most ambassadors as personal representatives of the President—they usually take directions drafted by an assistant secretary or below. No purpose is served in perpetuating the fiction.

To be sure, some ambassadorships to countries whose relationships with the United States are of overriding importance are of a different order. Usually in those cases, a web of political, cultural, economic and military connections makes appropriate an American envoy who actually is the personal representative of the President rather than merely of the State Department. Fifteen or twenty ambassadorships would, therefore, be reserved for presidential appointments confirmed by the Senate, and could be used by the President as he wishes for those countries he and the Secretary regard as falling within that category. These need not be assigned to the largest nations; one can visualize a particularly sensitive negotiation, like that over the Panama Canal, which could require an ambassador-at-large or an ambassador to a small country drawn from this pool. . . .

A careful examination of presidential appointments in the Department should also be made with an eye to converting any that should

---

[7]Under the Foreign Service Act of 1946, *all* Foreign Service officers like military officers are presidentially appointed with the advice and consent of the Senate—to a class or grade, rather than to a specific post (22 USC 906). . . . Because Foreign Service officers are presidentially appointed and confirmed for all promotions, it is clearly not constitutionally required that they be nominated and confirmed to each ambassadorial job assignment, as is statutorily required today (22 USC 901).

not be regarded as truly policy-level positions into career appointments of the Secretary. The rest, particularly assistant secretaries and above, like the small group of political ambassadors, will be the President's men and women.[8] This doesn't mean that Foreign Service officers would be ineligible for appointment to these positions; that, too, might be an unconstitutional abridgement of the President's appointment power. But—and it is a very big but—the law should require any Foreign Service officer who accepts such an appointment immediately to resign from the Service with no right of return. On those rare occasions in the past when a civil servant accepted a presidential appointment, that has been the practice in other departments[9] and it should be the rule in the State Department. Once having accepted a presidential appointment, a career officer should have committed his or her fortunes and loyalty to that President's administration. If the appointee has the right to return subsequently to the Service, either that commitment and the resulting presidential confidence will be undermined, or else subsequent administrations would be disadvantaged. . . .

If this proposal were made law, what benefits would flow from its implementation? Foreign policy formulation would thereafter be generally recognized as the responsibility of political authority and, at least conceptually, would be distinguished from foreign policy execution. The latter responsibility, clearly subordinated to the former, would be the task of the careerist. A clear line of demarcation between political appointments and career jobs would, both at home and abroad, substantially lessen that institutional friction between the Foreign Service and the presidency which has negatively affected the conduct of American foreign policy.

The Foreign Service would have gained a great deal, however: a fixed number or percentage of ambassadorships—the vast majority, at that—would be reserved to the careerist. What is crucial here is not so much the particular number, but that there be a fixed number.

---

[8]A limited number of political appointments below the rank of presidential appointment would be necessary as immediate staff to presidential appointees, corresponding to the "Schedule C" or NEA appointments in other departments. These are now generally treated as Foreign Service Reserve appointments, but I would suggest a separate category to avoid needless friction. Perhaps one top administrative post could be reserved for a careerist who would then be recognized as the senior serving Foreign Service officer, but I do not see this post as carrying a line policy role like the Under Secretary for Political Affairs.

[9]Unfortunately, the Civil Service Reform Act of 1978, effective this July [1979], provides otherwise. . . .

Certainty as to the number of political appointments would substantially relieve the quite natural career anxieties of Foreign Service officers; future political appointments would not thereafter be seen as the institutional threat they presently constitute. Furthermore, with only a relatively few ambassadorships to appoint—at senior levels—any President would be a good deal less likely to give those appointments to men and women whose primary qualification is financial campaign contributions.

Most important, as Presidents gained greater confidence in their ability to control the Foreign Service, they would have less incentive to circumvent the State Department. The undoubted expertise in that Department, therefore, would be more effectively employed.

The Ambassadorial Issue: Professionals or Amateurs?

Clare Boothe Luce

A public controversy has arisen concerning the conduct of our foreign affairs, namely whether amateurs or professionals should be appointed to head our embassies abroad. If we are to examine the issue seriously, we must agree not to prejudge it by using the terms "professional" or "amateur" in any deprecatory or pejorative sense, such as equating them with "cookie-pushing" and "pin-striped pants" on the one hand or "bungling" and "political payoffs" on the other. Amateurs are frequently called upon to wear pin-striped pants and professionals have been known to bungle; and in the intramural politics of the State Department, no less than "on the Hill," there have also been "political payoffs." If the issue is valid, we must discuss the merits of the amateur ambassador as opposed to the merits of the professional.

Certainly it will readily be agreed that a man who has made the practice of diplomacy his life work, his only career, can be called a "professional." We can also agree that the term "amateur" may then be used to designate a man who has come into diplomacy from any other walk of life, and who does not intend to pursue it as his profession or career. We may further agree that an "amateur," that is to say a non-career man, who has worked closely with professionals over a period of years—who has, for example, served in the State Department, the non-career missions attached to our embassies, or other branches of government where he has acquired a wide and practical knowledge of foreign affairs—might fairly be classed as a semi-professional, or in the language in which the professionals themselves classify him, as a "foreign expert." Defined in these terms, the issue of "amateur versus professional" is a relatively new one, for the reason that a realistic choice between the professional and the amateur ambassador has existed only in recent times. . . .

Plainly, when the ambassadorial question is raised solely in terms of a categorical choice between "amateur" and "professional," the issue seems to settle itself: the skilled practitioner of the art of diplomacy is clearly to be preferred to the novice; the diplomatic "generalist," or "trained political specialist with a knowledge of everything," to the untrained neophyte. When we further consider that the very survival of our nation, in this age of the hydrogen bomb and atomic weapons, depends on the success of our multitudinous, worldwide diplomatic undertakings, can any other answer be reasonable or prudent? Is it not, therefore, desirable—indeed vital—that our professionals, who are now fortunately available, should be put in charge of all our embassies, especially in sensitive areas where the lack of diplomatic skill, not to mention a "blooper," might endanger the success of our policies, perhaps the security of the United States itself?

With these definitions, and with these dangers well in mind, let us leave the field of argument to survey the field of facts. . . .

Certainly [a] review of the facts concerning the numbers, and whereabouts, of our amateur versus our professional ambassadors should remove any sense of public alarm or urgency which may today surround the issue. Two-thirds of our ambassadors are already professionals, and many of the remaining amateurs can be classified as semi-professionals and foreign experts.

These facts, however, do not invalidate the real issue—namely, *in principle* should United States Missions abroad be headed by professionals or amateurs? Is there any room for amateurs, even for those who have, in the course of time, become "experts" in American diplomacy? We cannot answer this question without widening the focus of our argument, by asking what room the American system, and the American Constitution itself, make for the "amateur diplomat."

The room that the Constitution itself provides is the President's room in the White House, and the Secretary's room in the Department of State.[1] The Constitution designates the President as our number one American diplomat. Throughout our history all our top diplomats have embarked on their great appointed task of formulating and carrying out our foreign policy as "amateurs." The Constitution also permits our number one diplomat, the President,

---

[1]The statutory basis for this responsibility lies in the Act of Congress, July 27, 1789.

personally to pick our number two diplomat, that is his Secretary of State, from any walk of American life he chooses. The President is similarly empowered to appoint, with the advice and consent of the Senate, all our diplomats to foreign countries who are then sent abroad as the President's *personal* envoys.

Any comprehensive list of the Presidentially appointed amateurs who have been sent throughout our history to negotiate for the United States abroad, and who have done so with distinction, would be far too long to include here. One can only mention the names of a few amateur envoys of the past: Benjamin Franklin, Thomas Jefferson, Gouverneur Morris, John Jay, James Monroe, John Quincy Adams, Albert Gallatin, Washington Irving, John Hay, James Russell Lowell, Joseph Choate, Jacob Gould Schurman, Myron T. Herrick, Richard Washburn Child, Lewis W. Douglas, Admiral William Harrison Standley and General George Marshall—all names first associated in the public mind with achievements outside the field of diplomacy.

Nor can we limit the room made by the Constitution for non-professional diplomacy to the President, the Secretary of State or the President's personal envoys. Every United States Senator and Congressman functions at one time or other—and these days with increasing frequency—in the field of foreign afairs. Legislators who set about, by voice or vote, to support, amend, cripple or destroy the foreign policy of any given administration are profoundly affecting the conduct of our relations with foreign countries. They are, in the true sense of the word, foreign policymakers. One has only to consider the impact abroad of certain resolutions (*i.e.,* Suez, Formosa), immigration and tariff bills, and the vast complex of foreign affairs legislation and appropriations, to realize that in the final analysis our amateurs in the Congress have more influence on the foreign affairs of the United States, and wield more "diplomatic" power, than all the practitioners of "organized diplomacy" put together. In our constitutional democracy, the members of the Congress, amateurs all, are empowered to play a decisive part in the nation's diplomacy. As a result of the increased speed of communications, and the necessities of American foreign policy, many of them have now become familiar figures in our embassies and in foreign chanceries. . . .

We must also take into account the amateur diplomacy practised by the million or more Americans who visit, live or work in foreign lands: the American businessmen, creating better and more abundant commercial relations; the scholars, artists, lecturers, students, creating wider and deeper cultural relations; the agricultural experts, scientists, engineers and technicians, spreading American "know-how"; the news bureau men, constantly reporting to the home front on conditions abroad; the medical and religious missionaries, creating good health and good will among men; the hordes of American tourists who leave behind them a realistic impression of the American character; the organized groups of American labor men, spreading knowledge about the uses and practices of free trade unionism to the working men of other lands; the editors' groups, learning about foreign attitudes, explaining America's as they go; the members of our armed services, bringing the actual sense of America's solidarity with the countries where they are posted. All of these are "amateurs" (and I have listed only the most notable groupings) who are consciously or unconsciously assuming some of the tasks of modern diplomacy.

"It seems that . . . there is not only some room for amateurs in diplomacy, there is very great room indeed. Initially provided by the Constitution and sustained by the American tradition, amateur diplomacy is the American method. . . . Indeed, it is impossible to see how our democracy could conduct its foreign policy without the organized and unorganized assistance of amateurs."

More than 30,000 civilians are working for the United States Government abroad. Less than one percent of them are officers of the Foreign Service corps. . . .

But that is not all: even in the Service itself amateurs are now plentifully present. As a result of the "Wristonization" program of 1954, there has been a great influx of non-professionals into the ranks of the Service in all classes.

It seems that, under the American system, at least in the cold war world, there is not only some room for amateurs in diplomacy, there is very great room indeed. Initially provided by the Constitution, and sustained by the American tradition, amateur diplomacy is the American method, not only in the actual machinery, but in the theory which puts the machinery into motion. Indeed, it is

131

impossible to see how our democracy could conduct its foreign policy without the organized and unorganized assistance of amateurs. . . .

Where does the conclusion that amateur diplomacy is the American method leave the ambassadorial question? Closed? Not at all. It simply puts it into its proper perspective. It consequently permits us to raise the ambassadorial issue in realistic terms; namely, who should represent America abroad: the professional, the amateur, or the *best qualified man who can be found?* Obviously, the latter. And just as obviously, the reasonable presumption must be that the professional is most likely to be that man.

Certainly, *all other qualifications being equal,* in simple justice, the career man should be given preference over an amateur when an ambassadorial assignment is being made. He has spent his life in the Service, always a life of discipline and hard work, often of sacrifice and danger. If he has risen on merit close to the top of his profession he is entitled to reap its proper rewards, the prestige, the position, the power and the pay of an ambassador. Similarly, all posts, in all areas, should be as open to him as they are to an amateur.

It is natural and proper enough that the Foreign Service resents that this is not the case today. Of our 76 ambassadorial posts, career men today occupy *all* of the "hardship posts," while the non-career diplomats hold many of the easy, and *all* of the "plush," ones. That is to say, wherever you find a post where living and working conditions are inadequate and uncomfortable, where disease is rife or danger imminent, where strange customs and alien ways are practised, where it is too hot or too cold, too damp or too dry for the average American, there you will find not the amateur but the career man.

Life for an ambassador in a satellite country, and in many of the countries of Africa, the Middle East and Asia, can be worse than hard: it can be grim, ugly and depressing. Medical, hospital, educational and recreational facilities for American children range from poor to nonexistent. Social life is dreary beyond belief; American diplomats and their families in some parts of these areas can seldom enjoy, in their leisure hours, the normal pleasures of an American— restaurants, movies, sports or even visits to or from friends. Worst of all, vast distances, as well as dangers, give them the feeling of isolation from their fellow countrymen, and from America itself.

132

To be sure, in point of expenditure of energy, effort and work, the European posts are no easier than they are, say, behind the Iron Curtain. Indeed, in the big European posts an ambassdor's day is one of endless effort, sometimes to the point of exhaustion. But the honor, in the eyes of his countrymen, is greater. And life can be pleasant, stimulating, rewarding in Europe, especially for an ambassador's family. Where ambassadorships are concerned, we must admit that the professional often gets the skimmed milk of diplomacy, and behind the Iron Curtain the sour mash, while the non-career ambassador gets the cream. . . .

We have agreed that wherever an amateur is not *better qualified* than a professional for a top diplomatic job, the job should go to the professional. We have also agreed that the mere possession of money should in no way constitute a qualification. Obviously, neither should it constitute a disqualification.

We come now to the basic question: Are there any criteria equally acceptable to professional and amateur which we can use in determining the "better qualified man?"

What criteria does the Foreign Service itself set in rating its officers for promotion? . . .

We have only to review the above list [on an efficiency report form] of the human qualities desirable in a professional to see that these same qualities are equally valued in the non-professional. They are possessed in a greater or lesser degree by any man who has risen to eminence in public life, or who has made a notable success in any enterprise or profession which calls for continuous teamwork, and wide and fruitful contacts with his fellow citizens. . . .

Now a curious fact emerges from a study of the efficiency report: the great intangible assets that throughout the long history of foreign affairs in all countries have rendered envoys most effective in the art of diplomacy are not listed here. They are: prestige and esteem in the eyes of the diplomat's own countrymen, a proven interest in public affairs, a knowledge of political and economic realities at home and abroad and friendly contacts with leaders on the domestic scene.[2]

---

[2]In the words of a recent article by Walter Lippmann, "An appointment outside the career service . . . has to be justified by the special quality and the proved distinction of the candidate . . . [he should be] a man of demonstrable ability in public life." Harold Nicolson, in "The

When a man has acquired great prestige at home through his own successful and popularly esteemed efforts as scholar, banker, industrialist, statesman, publicist, businessman, public servant or humanitarian; when he has, over the years, demonstrated a lively and constructive interest in public affairs; when he has wide and varied contacts with other leaders on the American scene, and if in addition he enjoys the prestige that flows from a mutually valued personal friendship with the President or Secretary of State, such a man can certainly be called "a man of proven distinction," a Somebody with a capital S.

The prestige of a Somebody will give him the power to influence public opinion at home, to approach "key figures" without diffidence and make suggestions to them without impertinence. He will be a man who can "get things done" and "put things across" at home. And he will always get a warm welcome from the diplomats of the country to which he goes, who will view his appointment both as an honor to them and an opportunity to transact mutual business fruitfully and rapidly. And when such an ambassador arrives to take up his post, there is general rejoicing on the part of the professionals on his staff. After all that has been said, this is not as strange as it seems: the Foreign Service is a service dedicated, above all else, to the furthering of our country's objectives abroad.

As the constitutional right to appoint envoys rests squarely with the President, so, also, the prime responsibility for finding "the better qualified man" lies with him. . . .

Certainly there is a large measure of public agreement on what constitutes a "political payoff." In American political practice, the personal political convictions of an appointee; the size of his private fortune; the campaign contributions he has made in the past to the party of his choice; the private services he has rendered the party; his personal relation to key figures in government (such as his blood relationship, friendship or business association with them)—all are considered to be circumstances which *as such* neither qualify nor unqualify him as a candidate for any high office. But when these same circumstances are presented as being *qualities* or *virtues* of the candidate's person; especially when they seem to be his *only*

Evolution of the Diplomatic Method," writes that "the Greek cities were constantly sending and receiving ambassadors of a temporary, or *ad hoc* character." These ambassadors "were chosen for their known respectability, and reputed wisdom."

qualifications for the job to which he aspires, it can be assumed—and the assumption is generally a valid one—that the appointee is a "political payoff."

In view of the President's constitutional right to appoint whom he pleases, his appointments cannot be prevented. But, fortunately, the Constitution itself provides a recourse against the assumption of office by such men: the Senate has the power to *disqualify* them. It has the right to refuse to confirm their appointments.

In passing, let me say that although it is conceivable that legislation could be drawn to prevent their designation, in the first instance, by the President, it would be very difficult indeed to draw such legislation in view of the many reasons listed above why they are, in political practice, "paid off." Often the least of these is "the size of the campaign contribution." A "crony" of somebody high in government always has an inside track over the campaign contributor. Moreover, if the Senate fulfills its duty—which is to refuse confirmation of unfitted candidates—such legislation is obviously unnecessary.

Not only in recent years, but also in the past, the Senate Foreign Relations Committee has failed in this, and even while "leaking" opinions from its secret hearings about the unfitness of some ambassadorial candidate, has proceeded forthwith to confirm him. It is this fact which makes subsequent charges of "political payoffs" both specious and hypocritical.

Such failures on the part of the Senate Foreign Relations Committee tend to prove that too many of the Senate's members—Opposition no less [than] Administration—still regard ambassadorships as a part of the political spoils system; and that the chief motive underlying their charges of "payoff" is the desire to embarrass the President and the party in power in order to score a party advantage in future campaigns. This suspicion is especially justified when—as is the case today—the Opposition controls the Senate Foreign Relations Committee, and with it the power to refuse confirmation to an Administration candidate.

The Senate would do well to remind itself that the public today ardently believes that whatever room there may be for amateurs in modern American diplomacy, there is no room for the kind of amateur who was once graphically described by a Congressional friend of mine as "an unknown public nonentity." When the Senate confirms a man who, in the considered judgments of a substantial number of the Committee, is not qualified to represent America abroad, it is doing an unpatriotic act. An ambassador's prestige, when he arrives in a foreign country, is America's prestige. And obviously, when members of the Senate Committee set about to damage the reputation of a qualified man in order to secure some slight party advantage, the action is unpatriotic.

The responsibility for preserving and increasing American prestige abroad, as it is reflected in the calibre of our "Ambassadors Extraordinary and Plenipotentiary," is the dual responsibility of the President and the Senate. As concerns the rôle of the President in this connection, I might quote the words of Mr. James Reston in *The New York Times* of August 7 [1957]. "The issue is not," he wrote, "whether the Eisenhower Administration is being more political in its ambassadorial appointments than the Democrats, or whether these jobs should be given to the top career men in the Foreign Service, but whether the appointments have met the President's principle of appointing the best man available, regardless of party, wealth or foreign service record."

As concerns the Senate, I might quote Senator Hubert Humphrey, who led an important and illuminating debate on this subject in the Upper House on August 15: "Let us have a little more public discussion of nominations when they come to the committee. I think all of us have been slightly derelict." . . .

An Ambassadorial Quota System (S. 1886)

John Krizay

Of all presidential appointments, ambassadorships are probably the most carefully scrutinized and widely criticized. The exalted title, the exotic social life of top diplomats, and the aura of elegance that surrounds the ambassadorial role supposedly make these appointments particularly attractive to well-heeled campaign contributors whose only qualifications are wealth and party loyalty. Although few ambassadorial positions are truly glamorous today, and although the percentage of non-career ambassadors has steadily diminished during the past thirty years, the career Foreign Service has maintained a steady drumbeat for a larger, guaranteed share of ambassadorial positions.

Senator Charles McC. Mathias, Jr. (R-MD) has long been an advocate of the Foreign Service view. Since 1974, he has initiated various legislative proposals to put a ceiling on the number of ambassadors the president may appoint from occupations outside the career ranks. His most recent effort in this regard, S. 1886, would amend the Foreign Service Act of 1980 by limiting political ambassadorial appointments to 15 percent of the total of such positions.

The Debate. The case for a statutory limit on non-career ambassadorial appointments rests on two arguments: 1) that it would create additional opportunities for advancement within the Foreign Service, thus enhancing morale and incentive; and 2) that ambassadorial appointments from the career service are likely to be more highly qualified than non-career appointees.

It is argued that young, upcoming Foreign Service officers become discouraged about their own chances of ever moving up in a Foreign Service that leaves so many senior officers idle at the State Department while the best diplomatic positions are filled by outsiders. The most capable middle and upper middle-grade FSOs, it is alleged, leave the service prematurely because political appointments leave

From The Heritage Foundation Issue Bulletin No. 85 (Washington, DC: The Heritage Foundation), June 3, 1982. Reprinted by permission.

no room at the top for careerists. That the oversupply of senior officers may stem from other causes is not addressed by proponents of S. 1886, nor do they indicate how many senior FSOs are underemployed or how many of them would be absorbed by the additional chief of mission positions S. 1886 would reserve for careerists. Simple arithmetic suggests, however, that the additional thirty or so slots this legislation might create would provide little relief if a surfeit of senior officers is indeed a problem.

The argument of the higher quality of career officers assumes that there is a professional component to the ambassadorial function that can best be acquired through years "spent in cross-cultural communication."[1] This component is never defined with any precision, although it is clear that it reflects the careerists' perception that an understanding of the interests and the *modus operandi* of other countries is more important to the conduct of foreign relations than an understanding of domestic issues that may pertain to international problems.

Even though they may concede that some of the most illustrious and competent ambassadors have been non-careerists, proponents of S. 1886 argue that a careerist, with years of exposure to foreign ways and foreign languages, is simply more "professional." Opponents of the measure argue that non-career appointees bring new ideas and approaches to the Foreign Service, which tends to be inbred and elitist, and that, in some instances, political appointees enjoy better access to the president, which enhances their influence with accrediting countries.

Underlying these two basic issues is a certain amount of pique over what many in the Foreign Service regard as an excessive number of appointments of "political" ambassadors by the present administration, interrupting, they claim, several years of steady progress toward a greater proportion of career appointments. The actual numbers, however, do not justify this concern. Of the ambassadorial posts now filled, 70 percent are held by career persons; 30 percent by non-career. The ratios have been similar for the last twenty years.

The Issue of Morale and Incentive. Foreign Service selection standards are probably more rigorous than those in most United States

---

[1]Martin F. Herz, "Who Should Be an American Ambassador?" *Foreign Service Journal,* January 1981.

government services. Even their strongest critics concede that Foreign Service personnel are generally superior to the personnel of other departments and agencies. The small percentage of applicants eventually accepted through such a demanding selection procedure, therefore, have high expectations of their Foreign Service careers. Morale problems occur when these expectations are not fulfilled. It would be a gross exaggeration, however, to attribute such dissatisfaction to the presence of a handful of presidential appointees in top positions. Morale has long been a problem at all levels of the Foreign Service officer corps, and, as such, the subject of much study. But the basis of the problem is not easily defined. There can be little doubt, however, that the decline in influence of the Department of State and the Foreign Service over the actual conduct of foreign relations during the last thirty years has been an important factor. . . . "Strong" Secretaries of State have managed to dominate major aspects of foreign affairs—mainly those having strategic implications. But, in exercising their dominance, they typically have relied on a selected few confidants—some from the career service, others not—while keeping the main body of the State Department bureaucracy at arm's length. . . .

Efforts to overcome the endemic problem of morale have focused on bandaid strategies rather than on instituting a structure that would enhance State's substantive output and thereby its influence. Inducements to early retirement, upgrading positions, and other gimmicks have been introduced as a way of stepping up promotions. One result has been an unhealthy obsession with job titles that has diverted the energies of too many FSOs from the real purpose of their careers. Over the past thirty years, with no increase in total personnel, the number of office directors has increased from under 40 to over 150; the number holding the title of Deputy Assistant Secretary of State has increased from seven to over sixty; ambassadorships have been created where no ambassadorial function exists.

Ostensibly, this title inflation has been developed to enhance the State Department representative's authority in dealing with other departments and agencies involved in the foreign affairs process, as if title alone could compensate for lack of substantive influence. In practice, however, the quest for titles has come to substitute for the rewards of work to the point where Foreign Service Officers resist any assignment not adorned with a title that exaggerates its importance. In a sense, this obsession with titles, and the State Department's willingness to pander to it, may be a major factor behind the persistent effort of the Foreign Service to capture a greater share of ambassadorial positions.

But increasing the number of career ambassadors could cause the morale problem to worsen. The turnover of many career ambassadorial appointments—especially in the smaller, hardship posts—is rapid. Because the system tries to give all deserving Foreign Service officers a chance at the coveted title, those leaving one post cannot always be reassigned as ambassador at another. Comparable titles thus have to be created to avert the appearance of demotion. This practice has become one source of the surfeit of senior officers.

It has been suggested that following service as an ambassador, the career officer be automatically removed from the ranks. Such a change in the system would have the double effect of making the career appointee more responsive to political leadership and moderating the surplus of senior officers insofar as that problem arises out of a need to find substitute top jobs for reassigned career ambassadors.

The Issue of Quality. No evidence has ever been developed to establish that career ambassadors, as a group, are superior to non-career ambassadors. Criteria for such evaluations are difficult to construct. The careerists' claim to professionalism and their argument that career Foreign Service officers are likely to outperform non-careerists stem from the FSO view of what constitutes competent conduct of relations. At one level, it must be conceded that those intimately involved in the operation know best. But the process of observing and dealing with other governments is only part of the foreign affairs mandate. Beyond the need to understand the policies of other governments lies the responsibility to the many businesses, unions, and other segments of U.S. society, whose interests are inextricably tied to events in other countries. The Foreign Service, however, devotes little time or attention to this side of the question.

Central to any analysis of this phenomenon is the incestuous nature of the Foreign Service personnel system. This elite corps of talented—even brilliant—men and women operates like an exclusive club, impervious to outside influence. Its system of selection, assignment, training, and promotion revolves around the subjective judgment of those who are already club members—all closely monitored and scrutinized by the most senior members who manage the club. In service abroad, where relationships are understandably very close, even social behavior and personal habits enter into the composite of impressions that influence recommendations regarding an officer's career.

"Non-career appointments to ambassadorial positions obviously are needed and can serve an important purpose. Anecdotes that focus on the incompetence of the non-careerist make for good copy in the press, but the career service, too, has produced inept and even embarrassing ambassadors. Tales of their ineptitude rarely escape the confines of the club."

This is not an atmosphere where bold new ideas are readily accepted or where departures from a traditional mode of thinking can flourish. The pressure to conform is particularly significant when it comes down to the kind of knowledge and talent thought to be suitable in a promising Foreign Service officer. Knowledge of obscure happenings in obscure countries is valued highly; events of greater importance in the United States are hardly considered. Members of this elite club may sneer at outsiders who cannot name the President of Zimbabwe while they, themselves, may be ignorant of the developments at International Harvester or Firestone and their implications for U.S. relations with important trading partners.

New ideas and, above all, reminders that all America has interests that extend beyond U.S. borders can come to this organization, as now structured, only through infusions of new personnel. With few exceptions, entry into the Foreign Service officer corps can occur only at the very bottom or at the very top. Those entering at the bottom quickly learn the virtues of conformity. Only those entering at the top can hope to infect the organization with some sense of the opinions and concerns of the entire nation and some willingness to accommodate the management of foreign policy to those opinions and concerns.

Non-career appointments to ambassadorial positions obviously are needed and can serve an important purpose. Anecdotes that focus on the incompetence of the non-careerist make for good copy in the press, but the career service, too, has produced inept and even embarrassing ambassadors. Tales of their ineptitude rarely escape the confines of the club. Criticisms of the non-careerist will almost inevitably be harsher, because he may bring to the institution an approach totally at variance with the traditional Foreign Service viewpoint. Innovations always run a greater risk of criticism and ridicule than safe, conventional ideas that deviate little from the established path.

The Issue of Numbers vs. Standards. President Reagan has appointed eighty ambassadors since his inauguration; forty-seven (59 percent) from the career service and thirty-three (40 percent) non-career. However, thirty-four ambassadorial posts have been left unchanged, and thirty-three of these are filled by career personnel. Since all ambassadors are obliged to submit their resignations when a new president takes office, there is no reason to consider those ambassadors who have been retained nearly eighteen months after the Reagan inauguration any differently than new appointees. The significant figures, therefore, are those that reflect the breakdown of career and non-career ambassadors now on the rolls: 70 percent career and 30 percent non-career. This is the same ratio that prevailed at the midpoint of the Ford Administration. At the end of the Carter Administration, one that gave heavy publicity to its interest in appointing careerists, the ratio was 71 percent to 29 percent.

The appointment process should not be judged only in terms of numbers, however. In a conceptual sense, it is possible to construct as strong a case for non-career ambassadors as for careerists. But there are no standards for judging the performance of past or present incumbents, and it is generally agreed that such standards are needed. Ambassador Carol Laise, former career officer and Director General of the Foreign Service, argued before the subcommittee hearings on the Mathias bill that there already exists "a very systematic process by which the Department identifies, assesses, and selects career officers for nomination by the President. . . . But, there is no comparably rigorous process today, nor has there ever really been in the past, for a review of appointments of non-professional people." This "systematic process" that applies to career appointees is nowhere defined for the public or even the FSO. The fact is that even career ambassadorial appointments are made on a highly subjective basis by a handful of people. The so-called "old-boy" network plays an important role in this personnel system where personal loyalties run strong and judgments are influenced by friendships and personal relationships that tend to become very close in the club-like atmosphere of Foreign Service life.

Most observers, including many careerists, would agree that the same objective standards should apply to the appointments of both career and non-career personnel. Former career ambassadors testifying on S. 1886 suggested a review committee similar to that employed by the American Bar Association in recommending appointments to the judiciary. Application of such a technique to ambassadorial appointments, however, would imply that the judgment of the foreign affairs community be paramount. A broader group might serve the purpose better. Its makeup should reflect the changes in the content of foreign relations in recent years—changes that make it impossible to segregate issues as purely foreign or domestic. . . . This situation has brought a new complexity to government-to-government dealings, which demands Foreign Service talents drawn from a broader—not narrower—professional background.

There is little evidence to support the contention that securing 85 percent of chief of mission positions for the career Foreign Service (as per S. 1886) would either enhance FSO morale or improve the quality of ambassadorial appointments. Sagging morale is more likely attributable to a decline in the State Department influence relative to other departments involved in foreign affairs. Offering the professional Foreign Service still more titles is unlikely to satisfy the desire for challenge that characterizes this select group of talented men and women.

As for the issue of quality, criteria by which ambassadorial qualifications can be judged have never been defined. This proposal employs the careerist's standard that an ambassador is judged by his experience with foreign cultures and languages. Another view holds that ambassadors should also have a thorough understanding of domestic issues and their increasing international implications. Moreover, the arbitrary restrictions of S. 1886 on the President's authority to appoint non-career ambassadors would deprive the Foreign Service of a major source of fresh ideas. Far from being beneficial to the interests of the professional Foreign Service, such a measure could cause it to become more inbred and more rigid in outlook with the result that the decline of its influence in the foreign affairs process would be accelerated.

7

In Favor of Career Appointments

It is not surprising that all three contributors to this chapter are career officers, now retired or, in the case of Ellis Briggs, deceased. The articles or excerpts represent unabashedly partisan positions and do not, except tangentially, address the principal arguments put forward in the preceding chapter. But they bring up many arguments which had not been considered, or were considered only tangentially by the authors in the preceding chapter.

The distinguished record of **Ellis O. Briggs** has been set forth in the introduction to Chapter 3. Reproduced here are excerpts from his book, *Farewell to Foggy Bottom*, published in 1964. **Malcolm Toon** was American Ambassador to Czechoslovakia, Yugoslavia, Israel and the Soviet Union. The article from which we reprint the first and last portions was originally published in the *New York Times Magazine*. The excerpt by **Martin F. Herz** from a long article in the *Foreign Service Journal* of January 1981 attempts to draw parallels between the diplomatic profession and the profession of medicine. Herz's career background was detailed in the introduction to Chapter 5. We express our appreciation to the publishers and copyright holders for permission to reprint.

This Is a Professional Game

Ellis O. Briggs

Ambitious young [people], entering the Foreign Service through a competitive examination so rigorous that it eliminates ninety-five per cent of the candidates, have a right to aspire to be ambassadors. To reach eligibility they will have had thereafter a minimum of two and nearer three decades of professional service in foreign countries and in the Department of State. Yet upwards to thirty-five per cent of ambassadorial posts still go to non-professionals, most of whom have no prior diplomatic experience.

Of the 111 posts recently listed by the State Department, only sixty-seven were held by professional ambassadors. And of the so-called normal posts—in contrast to the sixty-three "hardship posts"—forty-one per cent were occupied by non-professionals. The outsiders, that is, hold a higher proportion of the attractive world capitals than they do of those in malarial tropics, or bleak plateau regions, or other underdeveloped areas. In fact, the reluctance of some outsiders to take on tough assignments was illustrated years ago in a cartoon by Peter Arno. A hard-looking character is offering a pen to a fluttery campaign contributor with a checkbook; the latter is complaining: "But I don't want to be American minister to Bolivia."

Campaign contributors, across the years, have continued to prefer Switzerland, Ireland, and Denmark to Korea, Iraq, and Bolivia.

No single factor is more discouraging to those in the career service than the practice of awarding ambassadorial posts to non-professionals. It is especially disheartening when the beneficiary is either an outright purchaser or one whose claim to consideration rests on dubious or publicly weakened foundations.

The time has already overtaken us when it ought to be just as archaic for a President to dispose of a diplomatic mission as it would be, reverting to the usages of nearly two centuries ago, for him to sell a regiment or auction off a colonelcy. Moreover, it can be imagined what the effect on armed service morale would be if command of an Army corps, or of a fleet, were entrusted to an

From *Farewell to Foggy Bottom: The Recollections of a Career Diplomat* (New York: David McKay, 1964), ch. 3, pp. 36–48. Reprinted by kind permission of Mrs. Ellis O. Briggs.

un-uniformed outsider—to a Foreign Service Officer, for example. The infamy of it would be proclaimed from Bangor to San Diego, and the roof of the Pentagon would glow like the tail of a comet. Yet the reverse of this practice, equally abrasive to the morale of professional diplomats, is hardly an unusual occurrence.

Apologists for the non-professionals sometimes endeavor to divide them into categories. They would disqualify the candidate who comes, pocketbook in hand, to exchange a campaign contribution for a diplomatic mission. They would likewise reject the postulant who, having mismanaged the affairs of the Department of Agriculture or of the Thermal Dynamic Commission, is awarded an important embassy in order to guarantee his absence from the disenchanted Potomac environment for the balance of the administration. (Any Washington correspondent can identify specimens grown in that test tube.)

Those two categories of non-professionals are *bad,* say the apologists, and no more of them ought to be appointed. But there is a third group, they declare; they are the *good* non-professionals. During recent testimony before a Senate subcommittee, a former public servant expressed this thought as follows:

"In my own mind," he said, "I divide ambassadors into three categories. The professional, the Foreign Service Ambassador, who has risen to the top. I think the vast majority of ambassadorial posts should be filled by career officers.

"The second category would be the appointment of someone for services rendered, either financial or to a political party, and whose qualifications otherwise are not outstanding. I don't believe there should be any of those appointed. . . .

"Then there is a third category of ambassadors for whom I think there is a place. I think an outstanding man who has made a great success in other areas, whether it is the academic field or some other field, who has the talents and the abilities and perhaps special qualifications for a special post, I think there should be a place for them."

The witness then mentioned several eminent Americans who had in fact served their country well, in Bonn, Buenos Aires, London, New Delhi, and Paris. They are patriotic and civilized individuals, and no one familiar with their abilities could fail to be impressed by them. That, however, is beside the point. The point is that practically no outsider, however talented, can be so effective at representing the United States abroad as can the outstanding professional trained for the job—the officer who has risen to the peak of a competitive professional career and who has already proved in important missions successfully completed, his fitness for the topmost positions in the diplomatic service.

The Congress in 1955 established the rank of career ambassador to accommodate such officers and also to serve as an added incentive toward retaining highly superior talent in government service. The enabling legislation specified that no Foreign Service Officer would be eligible to be a Career Ambassador unless he had served at least fifteen years in a position of responsibility in a government agency or agencies, including at least three years as Career Minister (the next highest grade in the Foreign Service), and finally, unless he had "rendered exceptionally distinguished service to the Government."

The sights were set high by Congress in aiming at the top of the Foreign Service. Commenting on the establishment of the new grade, the *Foreign Service Journal,* unofficial publication of the diplomatic service, hailed the first selection of "our five-star professional ambassadors." Here is that first list, appointed by President Eisenhower in 1956:

James Clement Dunn entered the then separate Diplomatic Service in 1919.* Assistant Secretary of State, 1944. Ambassador to Italy, 1946; to France, 1952; to Spain, 1953; and to Brazil, 1955.

Loy W. Henderson entered the Consular Service in 1922. Director of the Office of Near Eastern and African Affairs, 1945. Ambassador to India, 1948, and to Iran, 1951. Deputy Under Secretary of State, 1955–1961.

H. Freeman Matthews began in the Diplomatic Service in 1923. Director of the Office of European Affairs, 1944. Ambassador to Sweden, 1947. Deputy Under Secretary of State, 1950. Ambassador to The Netherlands, 1953, and to Austria, 1957.

Robert D. Murphy entered the Consular Service in 1920. Personal Representative of the President in North Africa in 1942; U.S. Political Adviser on German Affairs with rank of Ambassador, Supreme Headquarters American Expeditionary Forces, 1944. Ambassador to Belgium, 1949, and to Japan, 1952. Deputy Under Secretary of State, 1953.

*The Diplomatic and Consular Services were separate until 1924, when the present American Foreign Service was established by the Rogers Act.

The experience of those four officers at the time of their appointment as career ambassadors totaled one hundred and forty years, or an average of thirty-five years for each. Each had been a career minister for a full ten years before his appointment.

In addition, mention should be made of the veteran diplomatist Jefferson Caffery, who, entering the diplomatic service in 1911, was chief of mission in six successive countries from 1926 until his retirement twenty-nine years later, just before the rank of career ambassador was established. . . .

"There remains one reason, more potent than the others, why the conduct of foreign affairs should be undertaken by professional diplomatists, trained in diplomacy. Political appointments are generally made for the good of the nominee, or the good of the dispenser of the patronage, or the good of the party in power. Professional appointments are made for the good of the country."

There is, alas, a . . . grouping of diplomatic representatives, before whom even the most charitable historian may flinch and throw his recording tablets into the river. Sample fauna in the *bad* ambassadorial menagerie include some very ripe specimens indeed. In deference to their descendants, their characteristics have been scrambled, so that identification will not be automatic.

There was the former chiropractor whose wife, mislaying a piece of jewelry during a reception, summoned the police and sought to have her guests—Cabinet ministers, fellow diplomats, and their ladies—searched before they were allowed to leave the embassy residence. Her mate was later apprehended attempting to smuggle art treasures out of the country, concealed in his diplomatic luggage.

There was Monkey-gland Archibald, the perpetual satyr, whose overworked hormones were still so hot that no embassy stenographer was safe, not even with his office door open. This antediluvian wonderman, senile and incompetent in other particulars, was the protégé of a politician so powerful that Archibald headed not one but two diplomatic missions before his arteries finally melted. . . .

And there was the horse doctor who fought with everybody, except maybe horses. When General Marshall became Secretary of

State he demanded from subordinates a count of chiefs of missions, with a view to disinfecting the list. Told that the veterinary was "the worst ambassador we have—anywhere," General Marshall next discovered that the political backing of the horse doctor was impregnable, and he could not be got rid of.

Not all these gaudy specimens were on the diplomatic racetrack at one time, nor focused in the binoculars of a single observer. But nearly every newspaper correspondent and American business leader abroad has a private memory stable where a stall is filled with equally spavined ambassadorial chargers, as good raw material for a glue factory as for a diplomatic mission. Even though the proportion of these spectacular emissaries to the total diplomatic population may be relatively small, their effect on the prestige and good name of the United States has been beyond computation.

Integrity, Prudence and Ability, indeed (as it says in the ambassadorial commissions).

Why have foreign governments put up with these people? These governments are quick to resent disparaging remarks or unfriendly behavior, but one of the hallmarks of a certain kind of non-professional is his naïve and ardent admiration for the country to which he is accredited, which he yearns to praise on every occasion. By assiduously cultivating this proclivity, by repeatedly calling the ambassador "Excellency," and by otherwise buttering up his diplomatic immunities, the Prime Minister is quickly able to get this amateur statesman into his pocket. To keep the American envoy there may be worth a tolerant attitude toward some of his extra-curricular activities.

Again, a foreign government is always informed about the antecedents of the American representative, including the amount and texture of his political backing. It may appear imprudent to jeopardize this American support by being severe with the ambassador at a time when for instance, a foreign-aid melon is about to be apportioned.

Or the foreign government may simply be discouraged at the possibility that the successor to Monkey-gland Archibald, should he be declared *persona non grata,* might turn out to be a dentist from Itching Springs, Oklakota, with a penchant for mixing laughing gas with the bourbon and serving it instead of champagne at his dinners. That government accordingly assigns a professional diplomat from its own service to Washington and handles its business through him, instead of through the American embassy in its own capital. Monkey-gland Archibald, no longer summoned to the Foreign Office, is happily able to extend his researches beyond the desk-tops of his own chancery. The business of the foreign government with the United States—in contrast to the business of the United States with the foreign government—is adequately protected. The only losers are the American government and people.

In deference to the present situation and perhaps also to the spirit of progress, it may be observed that most non-professional ambassadors are trying to do their best, and that there are possibly fewer bad non-professional representatives than there were, say, a generation or even fifteen years ago. But the breed is by no means extinct. And today the stakes are infinitely higher, so that the prospect of wear and tear, damage or loss to the national purposes—to say nothing of the national heritage and ideals—is greater than ever.

It is thus a shameful thing that the American government, for the greater satisfaction of a handful of politicos of the dominant party, goes on handicapping itself in its dealings with other nations.

There are several reasons why few amateur ambassadors can compete on even terms with professional Foreign Service Officers who have risen to be chief of mission. The most obvious is that the newcomer lacks experience in the practical functioning of diplomacy. The atmosphere is strange to him. The tools are new to his hand and often seem oddly shaped. The terms of reference are different from those to which he is accustomed. Granted that by its nature diplomacy is an imprecise business (although its purpose is the rendering of precise agreements that will endure between countries), there is nevertheless a feel for and a familiarity with it, acquired by skilled operation of the machine of foreign affairs and in no other fashion.

A professor has declared that the three elements of diplomacy are *persuasion, compromise,* and *threat of force.* Very well. Assuming that this oversimplification is true, where is the textbook or teacher who will tell the would-be diplomat how to blend these ingredients for use in a given situation?

How much persuasion is enough? When do you introduce even so little as the faintest whiff of the potent additive of threat? And compromise, when do you start compromising? How far can you safely tiptoe down the compromise path that for so many has suddenly become a roller-coaster, just around that safe-looking corner?

And when do you produce the threat itself, in all its hairy-chested menace? When do you tell those gentlemen across the table from you: "OK, boys. This is it. Take your muddy galoshes off my national doorstep—or else!" (And what do you do when one of them answers, "Horsefeathers . . ."?)

Furthermore, no two situations are alike. The mixture of tactics that produced that fine eupeptic effect on the negotiations last Thursday may act as a narcotic or conversely as too powerful a propellant if used on a problem arising the following Tuesday. In fact, almost the only thing that is predictable about diplomacy is its unpredictability. That is one of the things that a Foreign Service Officer learns day by day and year by year as he progresses through the grades of a competitive service. That is one of the things that cannot be learned overnight, not even by the most gifted amateur envoy.

A less manifest reason for the superiority of the professional over the volunteer is that the latter rarely realizes that personal popularity is not essential to successful ambassadorial performance. Popularity is like the olive in a martini; it's all right if you happen to like olives, but the martini drinker can easily survive without them, and an olive displaces some of the gin.

Respect, not popularity, is the essential ingredient in diplomacy. That is especially difficult for a politician-turned-diplomat to accept, for without enough popularity to swing the votes, even the statesman-politician soon finds himself on the domestic mulchpile. Consequently a political ambassador is often convinced that cultivating his public-relations garden is the most important activity in which he could possible engage abroad. . . .

In Washington I once had occasion to survey the effectiveness of American representation over a period of years in one of the most important capitals of Latin America. Two ambassadors had performed there more competently than the rest. One was feared more than he was liked, and the other received little acclaim from foreign officialdom or press. Each proved a successful envoy, for each was *respected*. In contrast, the most popular American ambassador ever to serve in that capital, without whose genial presence no party was ever complete, accomplished virtually nothing.

That is not to say that *un*popularity is a gauge of success in diplomacy, or that ambassadors ought to go around like Cyrano de Bergerac, exclaiming: "Here comes, thank God, another enemy!"

152

It is merely to observe that there are factors other than the approbation of foreigners that enter into profitable diplomatic achievement.

An ambassador is an appointed official. Moreover, he is not accredited to the *people* of a foreign country but to their *government*. . . . What the foreign government is trying to find out is what the United States will do if the tariff on frozen poultry is raised, and what it wants from the American representative within its gates is dependability and accuracy of judgment in reflecting the Washington point of view—just as the American government values the same attributes in the foreign diplomatic representatives assembled in Washington.

Respect, not popularity, is what counts in diplomacy.

It takes time for these things to be learned. Thus the intelligent non-professional, if he remains a diplomat longer than most members of his class are willing to serve abroad, could conceivably end by being a fairly successful representative, beginning four or five years after his appointment. But why our government should be conducting a training course to convert amateur diplomats into professionals, when it already possesses a corps of professionals whose training has long since been accomplished, is not always easy to comprehend. . . .

There remains one reason, more potent than the others, why the conduct of foreign affairs should be undertaken by professional diplomatists, trained in diplomacy. Political appointments are generally made for the good of the nominee, or the good of the dispenser of the patronage, or the good of the party in power. Professional appointments are made for the good of the country.

In Defense of the Foreign Service

Malcolm Toon

. . . Despite shuttle diplomacy and summitry and instant communications, the ambassador's role remains an important one, and any country with important interests abroad—such as the United States—requires high quality in its foreign representation. The ambassador may be an endangered species, but he need not be obsolete or even obsolescent, provided he is professionally qualified, respected by the leaders of both the sending and the receiving state, and given a significant role—at least in the tactical implementation of foreign policy, if not in its design and direction, where even the best of ambassadors can be only tangentially involved. In short, the ambassador, if the institution he represents is to survive as a useful adjunct of national policy, must be good, and he must be used.

This has not always been true of our ambassadors, and it is not true of too many of the people who fill our top foreign diplomatic posts today. Because of our practice of assigning a high proportion of our diplomatic missions to friends and supporters of an incumbent President, we continue to flog our friends abroad—and adversaries as well—with undistinguished appointees. In the process, our image is tarnished, and our sensitivity to changes in a foreign nation's mood and attitude is diminished. One consequence is to weaken our ability to formulate and implement rational foreign policies designed to advance rather than impede the national interest. And, worse, at times we look inept, bumbling and even ridiculous. As a concerned American citizen, I feel strongly that the United States of America cannot afford to look silly anywhere, anytime, on any issue. . . .

There is a reason, of course, why we have a system of choosing ambassadors that is strange to most of our friends abroad and almost unique among nation-states, and that is our singular historical experience. As Senator Charles McC. Mathias Jr., the Maryland Republican, wrote last April in the *Foreign Service Journal,** we decided

---

From the *New York Times Magazine*, December 11, 1982. Reprinted by kind permission of the author.

*[Reprinted in Chapter 5 above.—Ed.]

to make a clean break with most of the institutions of British tyranny when we achieved our independence, and one of the first to go was the European diplomatic practice. . . . "The first American diplomats were consciously chosen from the mainstream of American life and . . . returned to other careers following their diplomatic service." It is noteworthy that some of our early Presidents—both of the Adamses, Jefferson, Monroe and Van Buren—put in stints as American envoys. With such outstanding statesmen serving as our principal diplomats abroad, it is understandable that in the formative years of the Republic a legacy was built up, providing strong support for the thesis that a professional diplomatic service was neither needed nor desired. This—along with an increasing tendency to favor the President's friends and political allies for the choice assignments—remained the pattern of the diplomatic appointment process throughout the 19th century. . . .

Gradually, our initial national prejudice against professional diplomats eroded; the process was helped by the high incidence of corruption and incompetence among our mission chiefs in the 19th and early 20th centuries. And we as a nation began to see advantage in a career service based on merit. The result of this change in the national mood was the passage of the Foreign Service Act of 1924, which established the career diplomatic service and placed emphasis in ambassadorial appointments on ability to perform rather than on contributions to political party coffers. The percentage of career diplomats as chiefs of mission—i.e., those in charge of our diplomatic establishments, whatever their rank—gradually increased, attaining an average of 70 percent in the post-World War II period.

But the spoils system has by no means been eradicated. The current roster of ambassadors abroad makes that uncomfortably clear. [Examples deleted.—Ed.] . . .

Some would say—and in fact have so expressed themselves, rather indelicately, in my view—that as a former career diplomat I am subjective in my attitude. I can't quarrel with this charge; certainly one who has spent most of his adult years in the Foreign Service must inevitably have his judgment and outlook colored by his experience. While I may legitimately be accused of career bias, others who agree with my complaint cannot be so charged.

For example, in his recent article on the subject, Senator Mathias pointed out that of 14 new ambassadors appointed to the capitals of the Western alliance, 10 were political appointees; that the same is true of 14 of the 18 ambassadors named to member states of the Organization for Economic Cooperation and Development; that a political ambassador has just been named to [deleted], and that only one of four new ambassadors in the Caribbean area is a career diplomat. The Senator, who has sponsored a bill to limit political appointments to 15 percent of the number of ambassadors serving at any one time, adds that while some of the current political appointees will no doubt make excellent ambassadors, "it is hard to understand why there is so little room for career officers in these areas."

It is equally hard to understand why career professionalism is being short-changed in other sensitive areas. A random sampling of views expressed to me by foreigners friendly to the United States will reinforce the point.

A Finnish diplomat on superpower representation in Helsinki: "It seems that your practice is to send us envoys whom we can't help but like but seldom respect, whereas the Soviet Ambassador traditionally has been an authoritative spokesman for his Government but personally obnoxious."

"So, for two basic reasons, we must modify the way we appoint our envoys: To insure that our ambassadors are top-drawer, and to attract and retain in the Foreign Service the best and the brightest of our young people. While we cannot realistically expect any President to agree to a complete exclusion of his friends and supporters, surely we have the right to expect a President to be more judicious in his selection of envoys."

Yitzhak Rabin, the former Israeli Prime Minister, at my farewell reception in Tel Aviv, before my successor as Ambassador to Israel had been named: "Tell Washington to send us another professional—one who can report accurately and objectively on our views and who is informed on and can articulate Washington's concerns."

A Canadian commentator, when I spoke recently in Toronto: "If you Americans insist on lecturing us Canadians about the true nature of the Soviet threat, you should at least get your facts straight. Yugoslavia and Albania are not in the Soviet camp."

What I have said so far, it seems to me, adds up to the following: We must strengthen our representation abroad if we are to be seen as serious in our approach to foreign affairs. This does not mean that only professionals should man our embassies abroad. It does mean that our ambassadors, whether career or political, should be highly qualified, with a good understanding of the countries to which they are assigned, an informed appreciation of their own country's policies, and an ability to communicate—meaning a high degree of literacy and some linguistic competence. We must abandon our national mystique that anyone can be a good ambassador, if only he shares the ideology of an incumbent President, has demonstrated his loyalty by contributions to the party's coffers and understands— as a former admiral friend of mine once put it—"people" problems.

The story about the admiral is worth telling. When serving as Ambassador to Czechoslovakia, I, as an old Navy hand, was invited to sail with the Sixth Fleet. Before joining the carriers, I dined with a senior admiral in Naples who, after dinner, informed me that he faced retirement, would seek another career, since he was still "young and vigorous," and thought he'd like to be an ambassador. I asked him why he thought he was qualified for the job. His answer was that ambassadors dealt primarily with "people problems" and he had been concerned with such problems his entire naval career.

I told the admiral that I, too, was contemplating retirement, was reasonably energetic and felt that I should seek a second career. I thought I could qualify for a naval command. The admiral blew his stack, and it helped little to calm him down when I explained that because of my five years in the Navy, with ample command and combat experience, I felt I was more qualified to take over a naval command than he was to take over an embassy.

The sequel to the story is that the following year he was appointed Ambassador to an important country in southern Europe, and I have yet to take over the Sixth Fleet.

In 1979, testifying before the Senate Foreign Relations Committee while still Ambassador to the Soviet Union, I said in a rather heated exchange with the ranking Republican member, Charles H. Percy of Illinois, that the country's interests would best be served by having all our missions manned by career ambassadors. On questioning, I admitted that, given the nature of our political system and the traditional modus operandi of our Presidents, this was unrealistic, and a more plausible goal would be to insure that all chiefs of mission, whether drawn from the career service or from the outside, be well qualified; that we should strive to appoint more David Bruces and fewer—preferably none—of those who are not able to name the Prime Minister of the country of their assignment or who are astonished to learn that there are two Koreas.

A tight limitation on the use of outsiders is basically why the leading countries of the world have strong diplomatic services; most rely heavily on the career principle, and only a handful of small, relatively unimportant countries follow our "spoils system." Why must we continue to be the odd man out? Now, more than ever, our country, as the leader and protector of the free world, has a crying need to be represented abroad by the best talent available. Now that we find ourselves in a world where we cannot impose our will on others; where we cannot revert to isolationism, even though most of us would be happy to rid ourselves of the mantle of world leadership; where, without the overwhelming military and economic power we once had, our options are limited, skillful diplomacy is more than ever the linchpin of our safety and that of the free world.

We cannot do the job with second-raters; we need the perceptive abilities, the negotiating skills and the communications arts that are the hallmarks of the seasoned, experienced professional. They may also, of course, be the attributes of the occcasional outsider whose experience extends beyond the manufacture of ladies' garments or the raising of Idaho potatoes and whose talents are not confined simply to a working knowledge of the English language.

Moreover, a change in our traditional way of doing diplomatic business is essential to the preservation of a strong, effective diplomatic service. Without a reasonable prospect of reaching the top of the career ladder, without some assurance that he or she, as a professional, will have the opportunity to make a significant contribution to policy formulation and implementation—in a word, without confidence that professionals will not be barred from positions of responsibility by an Administration's penchant for cronyism—the career officer, demoralized and deprived of hope, will throw in the towel, while those who might otherwise aspire to a foreign service career will seek other avenues of professional endeavor. In testifying last spring on the Mathias bill, Theodore L. Eliot, Jr., the Dean of the Fletcher School of Law and Diplomacy in Medford, Massachusetts, which has trained scores of Foreign

Service officers, said he was "acutely aware of how many officers we have lost or potential officers we were never able to recruit because of the perception and often the fact that ambassadorial posts for which they did or might train were closed off for political reasons."

So, for two basic reasons, we must modify the way we appoint our envoys: to insure that our ambassadors are top-drawer, and to attract and retain in the Foreign Service the best and brightest of our young people. While we cannot realistically expect any President to agree to a complete exclusion of his friends and supporters, surely we have the right to expect a President to be more judicious in his selection of envoys.

Surely we have a right to expect the President to be as mindful of the need to have the best available talent in diplomacy as, for example, in the judiciary. Presidents since Dwight D. Eisenhower have followed the practice of seeking the judgment of the American Bar Association on the qualifications of nominees for Federal judgeships. This precedent of review by a panel of distinguished lawyers may be the way out of the impasse

---

ASSASSINATED AMERICAN AMBASSADORS

James Gordon Mein
Entered Foreign Service 1941
Killed in Guatemala 1968

Cleo A. Noel, Jr.
Entered Foreign Service 1949
Killed in Sudan 1973

Rodger P. Davies
Entered Foreign Service 1946
Killed in Cyprus 1974

Francis E. Meloy, Jr.
Entered Foreign Service 1946
Killed in Lebanon 1976

Adolph Dubs
Entered Foreign Service 1949
Killed in Afghanistan 1979

caused by our Presidents' reluctance to say no to their pals, the Senate's traditional aversion to faulting a President on the quality of his ambassadorial choices, and the unlikelihood of getting the Senate to approve a numerical limitation on political appointments to diplomatic posts.

In fact, just such a proposal for a review panel was made by two former ambassadors in their testimony on the Mathias bill. As framed by one of them, John Wills Tuthill, a former Ambassador to Brazil, the proposal envisaged the creation of a bipartisan review board, composed of persons who have distinguished themselves in the field of foreign affairs.

In considering this proposal, we should dispose of a canard about our professionals that has been spread more widely and noisily by adherents of President Reagan than by any previous Administration in our time. I am talking about the assertion that political appointees are more reliable implementers of a President's policies because their loyalty is assured.

This charge takes two forms. One is the allegation that an entrenched elite of career diplomats in the State Department often works at cross purposes with the White House, seeking to frustrate a President's policies when it is out of sympathy with them. The reply to that is simple. A Foreign Service officer has an intellectual obligation to fight within the inner councils of government for policies he believes to be right, even if his recommendations go counter to the Administration's views. But once the President makes a policy decision, all Foreign Service officers must comply. If they feel they can't, they must resign. In my experience, noncompliance with settled Administration policy is rare.

There is also the broader and more sinister implication that Foreign Service officers who allegedly exploit their position to sabotage a President's policy are disloyal to country as well as to an incumbent Administration. This smacks of neo-McCarthyism, and, in my view, a return to the evil practices of that wretched period in our history would pose a real threat to the well-being and integrity of our Republic.

The claim that politicos are more reliable than professionals is not only self-serving, it is unfair, unfounded in fact and an insult to the Foreign Service. The career Foreign Service officer is professionally committed to President and country. As Charles S. Whitehouse, former president of the American Foreign Service Association, said in defending the service against these scurrilous allegations of disloyalty: "The commitment to a career of national service and the self-discipline which is required from the beginning permeates our professional ethic and infuses a spirit of loyalty to the nation and to its leaders." . . .

USING THE AMBASSADOR

. . . As I said at the outset of this essay, the ambassador must be good, but he also must be used. And when he is not used properly, the national interest suffers.

Let me speak to the point from my own experience. When, early in the Carter Administration, I learned, mostly from the press, that Washington was preparing its position on strategic-arms limitations for discussion with the Russians, I cabled Mr. Vance that it might be useful for me, as the Ambassador in Moscow, to return to Washington to participate in the formulation of our policy. . . . He suggested that I meet him in Brussels, where he planned to brief the NATO Council on his way to Moscow.

. . . [So] I journeyed to Brussels to meet the new Secretary of State. Mr. Vance asked me what I thought of our new strategic-arms proposals; I said I would be in a better position to reply if I knew what they were. He then briefed me on their contents, and when I told him they would be rejected out-of-hand by the Russians, Mr. Vance at first was incredulous, then discomfited and finally downcast. I was right—anyone with limited prescience and some knowledge of Soviet attitudes could have made the same prognosis—and real negotiations on SALT II were stymied for months.

Failure to consult ambassadors on their estimates of local reaction can frustrate, if not damage, the national interest. Equally, failure to inform the ambassador of Washington's moves affecting the country of his accreditation often leads to embarrassment and, worse, misunderstanding. Mr. Gromyko was incredulous when asked by one of my predecessors in Moscow about the current state of play in earlier SALT negotiations. "Do you mean Washington has not informed you?" the Foreign Minister asked. Finally, we should speak to foreign governments through our ambassadors abroad.

It is, perhaps, understandable, but not tolerable, that Secretaries of State since President Kennedy's day have succumbed to the wiles of Ambassador Dobrynin, who has been representing his Government in Washington for 20 years now, and have chosen to communicate with the Soviet Union through him rather than through their own man in Moscow. The result is that many important exchanges with Mr. Dobrynin have been inadequately recorded in Washington and sometimes not at all, while a full record, with Mr. Dobrynin's own gloss on it, is on file in Moscow.

I am convinced that if Washington insists on speaking to Moscow through Mr. Dobrynin—or his successor—misunderstandings of the kind that upset the final phases of the SALT II talks will continue to plague our relationship with the Kremlin. I would vastly prefer dealing with Moscow—or any capital, for that matter—through our man on the scene. At the very least, we should double-track everything through our missions abroad. And if our man abroad is well qualified—and the thrust of this essay is that he should be—our primary lines of communication with a foreign government, friendly or adversarial, should be through him, and the channel through that government's ambassador in Washington should be secondary.

Most of what I have been saying in this article bears on a vivid recollection I have of Mr. Vance's visit to Moscow in March 1977. When we met in the Kremlin with Mr. Gromyko, I noted the composition of our two delegations. Mr. Gromyko was flanked by seasoned experts, all but one with at least 20 years' experience in dealing with the United States, and all with broad negotiating background in arms-control issues. I then took a look at our team. In stark contrast, I was the only one who spoke the language and who knew something of the adversary we faced.

My hope is that the asymmetry symbolized by that lineup will be offset in the months and years ahead. This can be accomplished, however, only by using our professional talent to the maximum—above all, by drawing upon the experience and expertise offered by the American Foreign Service. Whenever we face the Russians across the negotiating table, or even on operational matters, we are confronted with complete professionals. Our national security demands no less from our side.

Who Should Be an American Ambassador?

Martin F. Herz

The question is not, and has never been, whether professionals or nonprofessionals ("political appointees") should be ambassadors. It is, rather, how one chooses or finds or trains the best people to become ambassadors.

"The best people?" Is there some undertone of *elitism* in that question? Yes and no. If it is elitism to want the best possible surgeon to operate, to want the fastest-running and highest-jumping athlete to compete, to have the best-trained and temperamentally best-suited man or woman as an astronaut, then it is elitism also to want the best man or woman available to represent the United States abroad. But of course it is not elitism in the snobbish sense that is sometimes imputed to that word. It is, rather, a rational recognition that difficult and responsible tasks should be performed by the most highly qualified people.

Certainly the United States—indeed, any country with important interests abroad—requires high quality in its foreign representation. It is only good common sense to want the most rigorously selected, best trained and most highly skilled people to man that first line of defense. But high quality is not a monopoly of Foreign Service professionals.

Also, it is understood nowadays that there are no "unimportant" posts to which one can assign unqualified or poorly qualified ambassadors. As I shall demonstrate, there is plenty of damage that an unqualified man or woman can do in such a post—and in today's world there is no guarantee that an American embassy in a quiet, out-of-the-way country may not suddenly become the focal point of American interests, perhaps in a wider regional context, which requires expert work of the highest professional quality.

What, then, do we mean by professionalism? Selection, training, experience, plus character and technical skills. If I distinguish between

Reprinted by permission from the *Foreign Service Journal*, January 1981.

"skills," which are highly important, and the factor of "experience" (which of course helps to develop and sharpen skills), it is because the job of an ambassador requires skills of several kinds, only some of which are transferable from other professions or can be learned rather quickly; and all of them are not always found in one individual. In recent years the managerial aspect of running a large embassy has become so important that executive experience, for instance the running of a large university, has come to be regarded as a qualification for running an embassy. Managerial skills are certainly more readily transferable than diplomatic skills.

This aspect of the question comes down to the one that has agitated also the medical profession (which I choose for parallels that could be cited with many other professions): Should a doctor or a managerial expert be in charge of a hospital? There are good arguments on both sides, but there is no argument whether a hospital administrator or a surgeon is better qualified to perform major surgery. In diplomacy, the manager of a diplomatic mission is also the surgeon who must "operate" in his conversations with the foreign minister and other elements of the power structure of the country to which he or she is accredited. He must make difficult diagnoses, and sometimes must prescribe (or recommend) risky therapy.

We have said that the managerial functions can be more easily delegated than the diplomatic ones. To come down to specifics: To appoint the governor of a Middle Western state to become United States ambassador to Mexico—a man who did not speak Spanish and had no background in foreign policy in general or Latin America in particular—would be about the same as to expect the governor of a South African province to perform, in the Groote Schuur hospital in Capetown, the heart transplant surgery that was previously performed there by Dr. Christiaan Barnard. With the difference that the nonprofessional diplomat has at his side a team that covers up for his mistakes and prevents as many as possible; whereas the unfortunate effects of bungled open-heart surgery are more quickly apparent. But it would be appropriate to make a governor who is a good executive the director of a hospital—on the understanding, of course, that he would leave the medical work to doctors.

What is it that makes a good diplomat, and thus a good ambassador, *in addition* to the factors that were enumerated above? The kind of empathy which comes from years spent in cross-cultural communication, *Fingerspitzengefühl* (the feeling one has in the tips of one's fingers) which is sometimes acquired by amateurs but is more frequently found among people who have had a great deal of experience. To use once more the medical parallel, there are diagnosticians who use all the apparatus of tests and examinations but make their most important decisions by intuition.

A gynecologist, for instance, has a patient who is brought to the hospital because of a suspicion of ectopic pregnancy, a potentially deadly complication. All the customary tests are made, and they are *negative*. The old professor and chief of the department, i.e., the old professional, says, "I think, nevertheless, that hers is an

---

"A 'feel' for what is about to happen may be derived from a lifetime of sniffing the political atmosphere of foreign countries. The crisis, which inevitably is the first diplomatic crisis to the newcomer, is reminiscent in many ways of crises experienced before by the professional—he knows what comes first and what not to worry about and is thus able to concentrate on what matters most. Inevitably, someone who has been through a dozen diplomatic crises behaves differently in one than someone who does not have that experience."

---

ectopic pregnancy. Take her to the operating room, we'll open her up." Which is done, and the patient turns out to have an ectopic pregnancy, notwithstanding the negative indications given by the tests. The old professor is asked how he knew. He doesn't know himself. But he has over the years seen tens of thousands of pregnant women, including large numbers whose pregnancies were ectopic. He could "smell" the symptomatology, including elements that were not tested but which probably had been present in previous cases that he had seen. Experience paid, and a life was saved.

The same very often holds in the field of diplomacy. The thing that is *not* present in the equation is noticed by someone who has learned to notice also what is not there; the inflection of the foreign minister in saying something signals an opening to the experienced professional which is missed by the amateur. An obscure reference to past history conjures up the memory of a useful precedent. The right tone, the right word, the right moment are utilized, not only by intellectual judgment but through familiarity with conversations of similar kinds in which things turned out right or went off the rails. A "feel" for what is about to happen may be derived from a lifetime of sniffing the political atmosphere of foreign countries. The crisis, which inevitably is the first diplomatic crisis to the newcomer, is reminiscent in many ways of crises experienced before by the professional—he knows what comes first and what *not* to worry about and is thus able to concentrate on what matters most. Inevitably, someone who has been through a dozen diplomatic crises behaves differently in one than someone who does not have that experience.

In other words, professionalism *pays*. One can, of course, appoint a businessman or politician to command an aircraft carrier or an armored division, and some may display gifts of strategic intuition which make a crucial difference—and most, being surrounded by professionals, will make no fatal mistakes; but the chances of getting good results are greater if an aircraft carrier or an armored division is commanded by a man with specialized military experience. It can in certain cases be only *related* experience: Admiral Raymond A. Spruance, who had commanded battleships, made an excellent transition to a carrier task force; and some professors of international relations or diplomatic history have made serviceable ambassadors.

Of course it is true in all professions that some of its members have fallen on their faces even after rising up a career ladder and acquiring experience. But the odds are that people trained for the job will give better service than people who have not had such training and experience.

8

From Either Source, the Best

It should be noted that many authors, even while arguing for or against appointments from inside or outside the diplomatic profession, have taken the position that excellence can be found in both groups and should certainly be sought. The two contributions in the present chapter round out that point of view. One is written by a former senior diplomatic official who came from outside the career, the other by a former career diplomat. Both try to sketch out desirable characteristics and criteria. Neither is completely impartial, adhering to the view expressed for instance in the Jackson Committee report (Chapter 5) that non-career appointments should be the exception rather than the rule.

Gerard C. Smith, former head of the U.S. Arms Control and Disarmament Agency and chief SALT negotiator, chairman of the State Department's policy planning staff, and ambassador-at-large, writes on the qualifications for non-career ambassadors (which turn out to be not very different from those for career appointees). The contribution by **Martin F. Herz** represents the concluding portion of his article, "Who Should Be an American Ambassador?" of which the first section, which clearly favors career appointments, appears in Chapter 7. (The middle portion, which dealt with the appointment record of recent administrations, is not reproduced.) In his position as editor he is constrained to note that his concluding recommendations, here titled "Some Principles Regarding Appointments," still let his preference show. However, the suggested criteria are meant to be applicable to both career and non-career candidates.

Non-Professional Diplomats: Do We Need Them?

Gerard C. Smith

I will try to outline some criteria by which to judge the qualifications of non-professionals as chiefs of mission, and then I will give a few examples of individuals who, in my judgment, might be considered an all-American team of non-professional diplomats. But first I must make a confession.

I admit at the start that after some 33 years in or on the fringes of diplomacy, I have concluded that only in exceptional cases should the United States depart from accepted international practice by having an ambassador who lacks professional qualifications. Why is it unimaginable to place an aircraft carrier or a ballistic missile submarine under non-career command, or even under a naval reservist, while having a relatively large number of non-career appointees in charge of embassies where technical skills and experience are just as important? These positions can involve matters which are essential to the national security, but in a number of cases the U.S. has been represented by individuals whose main qualifications have been their contributions to political campaigns—of the past and those expected in the future. Such people are likely to be puppets, propped up and kept going by professional staff. They can be obstacles to carrying out a successful American foreign policy.

It is said that modern communications have largely eliminated any substantive role of a chief of mission, leaving the work for the most part representational. My experience in working with our ambassadors around the world suggests that this is not the case, and in the interdependent world of today skilled individuals of stature are still essential to diplomacy. But obviously there have been exceptions and there should be exceptions in the future. What, then, are the qualifications that we should look for?

Our non-career ambassador should be a man of stature who has made his mark in some important field of American endeavor, preferably involving service with the United States government.

He should have a warm personality and get along easily with non-Americans, work smoothly in a large organization (the State Department), be able to act with precision in accordance with instructions from Washington in dealing with the government to which he is accredited, have sufficient confidence to amplify them (properly labeled) where necessary to get across their spirit as well as the letter.

Naturally, absence of a good command of the language of the country is a substantial handicap.

He should have a bearing consistent with the dignity that a chief of mission needs—gravitas. He should command respect for the knowledge he has of the United States and the key issues of the day. His sympathy for the host country should not be blind. He should be able to speak well and not have to read remarks. Fate should have favored him with a charming and indefatigible wife. He should have unusual energy and stamina and be cool under stress.

He should be able to write with precision and have a working knowledge of the issues with which he will have to deal. He should be able to make judgments independent of the recommendations of his staff.

He should want to deepen his knowledge of and his skills in diplomacy.

He should not be a seeker after dignity and honor. As Ambassador Dwight Morrow once said, the important thing is to want to do something rather than to be somebody.

He must be able to work with cabinet officers and officials other than those of the State Department.

A good deal of his work will be not unlike that of an innkeeper and he must have the patience and skills to do that even though it may seem beneath his dignity.

He should get along well with Congressmen, both in Washington and with junketeers. He should have a flair for relations with the media.

He should have sufficient understanding of the problems of his region to be able to contribute significantly in regional meetings of chiefs of mission.

Since so much of international relations involves economics, he should not feel "at sea" in matters involving this dismal science.

If he is a person of wealth, he should not indulge the assumption that this random fact is any substitute for concrete qualifications.

Much has been made about the importance of political appointees having "clout" with the incumbent President. I think that this phenomenon, while important, is often exaggerated. A number of the criteria spelled out above are more important.

My candidates for an all-American team of non-professionals are David Bruce, Ann Armstrong, Mike Mansfield, Ellsworth Bunker, John Sherman Cooper, Douglas Dillon, John McCloy, Cabot Lodge.

Some Principles Regarding Appointments

Martin F. Herz

If we don't want the best, then nothing need be done. But if we do, we—the readers of this article and others who are concerned and wish to raise a voice in favor of upgrading the quality of ambassadorial appointments—can take into account some of the following considerations:

1. **Give Weight to Experience.** Career officers do not have a monopoly on qualifications for ambassadorial positions. However, experience in several Foreign Service posts and positions is more likely to point to such qualifications than experience in other work: Among ten candidates from the career service, the odds are that two or three may turn out to be weak or perhaps even misfits. Among ten non-career candidates, the odds are that the number will be considerably greater, especially if they do not come from fields closely related to foreign affairs. Experience counts—therefore, to the extent that potentially outstanding chiefs of mission can be identified early in their careers, to the extent that they can count on having more than one ambassadorship, the odds on developing outstanding ambassadors improve. Bringing along the most brilliant and competent officers to responsible positions in younger years—which is increasingly happening at present—gives the best promise of good results. The same is true, of course, of non-career ambassadors. Only the most outstanding candidates should be considered. Even then, if Thomas J. Watson, Jr., for instance, could have had prior apprenticeships as ambassador to Upper Volta and Bulgaria, he no doubt would have functioned considerably better in his position in Moscow.

2. **Consider Character.** Nicolson's dictum about character being the most important ingredient of a successful ambassador is still true. Yes, he also has to be an operator, but there is a distinction between skill in the organization game and cutting corners or buying favors or otherwise engaging in sharp practice. Moral courage is the first requirement of a good ambassador. It is found among both

Further excerpted by permission from the *Foreign Service Journal*, January 1981.

career and non-career candidates—but not as often as one might think. The idea that career people are too often "bucking for promotion" (or incentive pay) whereas non-career ambassadors are past such considerations is poppycock. Non-career ambassadors are sometimes more concerned about their "image" than they should be, and too often want so desperately to "succeed" that they violate Talleyrand's warning against excessive zeal. Case studies of ambassadorial failures on the job (career as well as non-career) would bring this out with telling conclusiveness.

3. **Beware of Vanity.** It is the greatest enemy of a good diplomat— and of a bad one, too. Even superb professionals have fallen victim to it, letting a personal slight, for instance, color their judgment of the person who administered it; or failing to report (or reporting inaccurately) developments which cast an unfavorable light on themselves. But vanity is found less often in a disciplined career service than among non-career people some of whom become light-headed when addressed as "excellency" and begin to suspect that they are omniscient. A career officer has learned the benefits of staff work and is more likely to listen to professional advice than a non-career appointee. Some of the most horrible gaffes committed by neophyte ambassadors occurred because of their unwillingness to use their staffs. I would be less than candid, however, if I failed to note that there have also been career officers in ambassadorial positions who lost their moorings, displayed symptoms of hypo-mania, and began to think of themselves as a combination of Jesus Christ, Talleyrand, and Napoleon. Such men—regardless whether career or non-career—must be swiftly brought down to earth, and home.

4. **Beware of Ethnic Appointments.** It is a fallacy to believe that appointing an American of Polish extraction (such as former Post-master General John A. Gronouski) to Poland will flatter the Poles; or that appointing someone of Italian descent (say, John A. Volpe) to Italy will flatter the Italians; or that appointing a black will flatter a black African country; or that appointing an American Hispanic (say, Julian Nava) as ambassador to Mexico will flatter the Mexicans. Whether they are flattered will depend on the qualifications of the appointee (quite aside from the question whether flattery is a good reason for any diplomatic appointment). If a Gronouski turns out not to speak Polish and a Nava turns out to know little about Latin American politics, the host country will be adversely impressed.

5. **And of Military Appointments.** The same goes for appointing a general to represent the United States in a country run either by a military dictator or by a political leader with a military background. When President Kennedy sent General James M. Gavin as ambassador to France, for instance, he no doubt thought that de Gaulle, being a general, would appreciate having an American general to talk with—but de Gaulle did not consider himself a general. He had nothing but contempt for "mere" generals, regarding himself to be far more, namely the embodiment of La France. Charles ("Chip") Bohlen, a man who knew European history backwards and forwards, spoke French fluently, and had met most of the European movers and shakers of the last thirty years, was a much more effective representative in France. He was also a more effective ambassador to the Soviet Union than any non-professional

---

"I would be less than candid, however, if I failed to note that there have also been career officers in ambassadorial positions who lost their moorings, displayed symptoms of hypomania, and came to think of themselves as a combination of Jesus Christ, Talleyrand and Napoleon. Such men—regardless whether career or noncareer—must be swiftly brought down to earth, and home."

---

could have been at that time. It is true, on the other hand, that a person of stature will run no risk of being overly impressed by persons of high rank; so there is merit in appointing to a major post someone who has rubbed shoulders with important people. Both career and non-career candidates can fill that requirement.

6. **Money Is No Qualification.** Should the possession of money (as distinguished from the payment of it) be a qualification for appointment to the large embassies where representational requirements are important? The answer is that the United States is wealthy enough to meet the legitimate expenses of ambassadors—and that it is doing so right now in most cases. *The Economist* a few years ago, noting that Ambassador Walter Annenberg had said that he spent $250,000 a year of his own money to live in London in the ambassadorial style he considered appropriate, and that he had

contributed $1.5 million to refurbish the residence, concluded that "there is no doubt that the job in London is expensive." Writing at that time under a pseudonym, since he was still on active service, the author of the present article suggested in a letter to the editor (printed in *The Economist* in January, 1973) that

> None of the expensive things that Mr. Annenberg did and which you list in your article seemed essential for the functions of an ambassador, unless you regard his giving of expensive gifts and his lavish entertaining as necessary for the conduct of diplomacy with your leadership. I cannot imagine why an American ambassador needs to prove to his guests by the opulence of his table or the number of footmen that the United States is a wealthy country.
>
> Suppose an American ambassador invited only 12 people to a dinner instead of 64—perhaps that would give him more of a chance to talk with his guests; and as for the maintenance of Winfield House I suppose that if the government had its choice between an ambassador who is an amateur but who keeps the grounds impeccably, or an experienced professional who allows them to run down a little, perhaps it would not follow your implied advice and would opt for the man of intellectual and professional substance, rather than pecuniary substance.

Meanwhile all this has been proven by the successful tenure of Arthur A. Hartman, a career officer with no private fortune, as ambassador to France. Elliot Richardson, not a career officer but also without a personal fortune, was not daunted by the financial requirements in London. Mike Mansfield, and before him Douglas MacArthur II and Edwin Reischauer, managed in Tokyo without the personal reserves expended by Robert Ingersoll. Chip Bohlen in Paris was able to make out, perhaps with some discreet support from the Department at a time when the House appropriations subcommittee was still especially niggardly with representation funds. In any case, the burden of proof is now on those who believe that one has to be wealthy to be ambassador in one of the world capitals. If I were given such a position and found it impossible to make ends meet, I would cheerfully cancel the Fourth of July reception in favor of more small luncheons and dinners—without any impairment of relations.

7. **Scrap the Board.** [This related to the Presidential Advisory Board on Ambassadorial Nominations established by President Carter which, in the author's opinion, "must be judged a failure." It has in the meantime been scrapped.]

8. **Wake Up the Senate.** The Senate, and especially its Foreign Relations Committee, has been derelict in not looking into the

qualifications of ambassadorial nominees and into undesirable reasons, such as political favors or campaign contributions, that might be behind their nominations. The information is available, in copious detail, that would permit at least a modicum of scrutiny to take place. It is not even necessary for this purpose that the examination of candidates be in great detail. Superficial examination, as the Gluck case and the gaffes of more recent appointees amply demonstrate, would bring out the most glaring lack of qualifications in a number of candidates. This, in turn, might lead to greater circumspection on the part of the White House and the political leadership of the State Department and would make them put the brakes on the kind of scandalous nominations that have been getting by without so much as a question. As indicated, the custom of "senatorial courtesy" is a problem. One way to solve it would be for the SFRC to adopt a rule whereby any of its members who have been recipients of money from a candidate should automatically disqualify themselves from consideration of his nomination.

Support the Chief. Finally, there is a question of the loyalty owed by the deputy chief of mission and the section chiefs and all the rest of an embassy's personnel to the ambassador who is, after all, the personal representative of the president and is entrusted with large responsibilities. This question has been raised in connection, for instance, with the publication by the *Foreign Service Journal* of a "whistle-blowing" article about the gaucheries, gaffes, and general incompetencies of an egregiously unsuited political appointee. The author of that article had been the ambassador's deputy. Is it right for such a man (or woman), whose very proximity to the chief of mission involves the sharing of knowledge in a position of personal trust, to lift the veil and reveal the feet of clay? In my opinion the answer is no, it is not fair, it is not right, it is an extremity to which one should resort only in desperate circumstances. Presidentially appointed chiefs of mission, even when they are incompetent, should be able to count on the loyal support and discretion of all their subordinates, and especially their DCM—unless it becomes *necessary* to tell the truth about their incompetence. As Winston Churchill wrote in connection with his appointment to become prime minister early in World War II:

> The loyalties which centre upon number one are enormous. If he trips, he must be sustained. If he makes mistakes, they must be covered. If he sleeps, he must not be wantonly disturbed. If he is no good, he must be pole-axed.

But this last extreme process cannot be carried out every day; and certainly not in the days just after he has been chosen.

In other words, loyalty to the chief of mission cannot be at the expense of the larger loyalty to the country and to those who govern it. Lest there be any misunderstanding let me make clear that "lifting the veil" on the chief has nothing to do with "lifting the veil" on policies with which one disagrees. An ambassador, or any of his subordinates, who believes such policies to be misguided has a duty to bring his views to the attention of Washington—and there are channels for this. But for the dialogue between Washington and the field to be constructive it must be confidential. "Whistle-blowing" or policy criticism in a classified communication to the Department of State is one thing, *public* disagreement with presidentially approved policy is quite another. Those who wish to disagree in public should resign and not expect to be protected by their career status against the consequences of indiscipline. Nothing that has been said about an officer's overriding responsibility to the country should be misinterpreted as recommending license to carry policy disagreements—whether within an embassy or between an embassy and Washington—outside the official family. The president must have continuing good grounds to count on the loyalty of every one of his appointees, and of course every Foreign Service officer (and every ambassador whether career or non-career) is a presidential appointee. The president must also be able to count on their discretion—and on their courage to speak their minds in confidential communications, because they owe the President their best judgments, regardless of how and from where they were appointed.

This, it seems to me, is the point that is too often missed when there is talk of ambassadors from inside and outside the profession. *All* of them are the President's men. Just as a flag officer or general officer in the armed services responds as a matter of course to the authority and leadership of the Commander-in-Chief regardless of the outcome of a particular election, so do all ambassadors (and other diplomatic officers) do the bidding and advance the purposes of our chief of state and government. Even to raise the question whether this is really so seems to them insulting.

9

Some Relevant Documentation

The Foreign Service promotion system uses a series of "precepts" drawn up for selection boards that consider the files of officers eligible for promotion. The year 1976 appears to have been the last in which separate precepts were issued for the selection of Class 1 officers to be promoted to the normally highest rank, that of Career Minister. (A still higher rank of Career Ambassador, corresponding to five-star rank in the military, was the subject of separate regulation. The first Career Ambassadors, appointed in 1956, are mentioned in the contribution by the late Ellis O. Briggs in Chapter 7 above.) We reproduce the 1976 Career Minister precepts because they indicate the desirable characteristics of a top-level diplomat as they were identified by the State Department. It is noteworthy that those characteristics include being "well versed in the current issues and problems of the American domestic scene."

The excerpts from the Foreign Service Act of 1980 provided here include only those sections that deal with the functions and criteria for appointment of chiefs of mission. The letter of May 29, 1961 from President John F. Kennedy to chiefs of mission is expressive of the broad range of authority granted such ambassadors. The document has had its counterpart in similar letters issued by succeeding presidents. Although the letter is primarily concerned with the scope of the ambassador's authority, it also provides insight into the multifarious activities of a modern embassy that fall under his jurisdiction.

Profile of a Top Diplomat

State Department Precepts

C. CAREER MINISTER QUALIFICATIONS

A Career Minister is expected to possess the ability, stamina and further growth potential to serve in key executive and foreign policy leadership positions in Washington and abroad. These include Deputy Assistant Secretary of State and above, Chief of Mission, Deputy Chief of Mission at a Class 1 Mission, U.S. Representative to an international organization, and similar top positions in the Department of State and other U.S. Government Departments and Agencies.

During earlier career development, a Career Minister would have developed top flight core functional skills, but would also have achieved some substantive and very likely area broadening. At some point in the officer's career development, a Career Minister would probably have had a detail to or worked closely with another department or agency such as Commerce, Labor, Treasury, AID, USIA, ACDA, or the Peace Corps (ACTION), which has major programs or is otherwise clearly involved in the international relations field. A Career Minister typically will have served overseas in a position of considerable responsibility such as Counselor of Embassy, Principal Officer at a constituent post, or higher. As a Class II or junior Class I officer, a Career Minister would normally have had responsibilities for foreign policy leadership requiring synthesis of the several functional areas.

It is likely that the Career Minister would have participated in the Senior Seminar in Foreign Policy or one of the War Colleges or another institute of higher learning for an academic year or longer.

More recent assignments would perforce have included Chief of Mission or one or more of the comparable jobs listed in 3 FAM 562.3. These could have been either overseas or in the Department of State—or perhaps in another U.S. department or agency.

A Career Minister will have demonstrated an unusual organizational and command talent. The officer's performance should be

---

From FAMC-721, Appendix A and B to the 1976 Foreign Service Selection Board Precepts, U.S. Department of State, October 13, 1976, pp. A4-A7.

noted for decisiveness; fairness in dealing with others; a willingness to delegate responsibility and authority; and especially an attention to the professional development of subordinates. A Career Minister should have a penetrating insight into the foreign affairs process, an outstanding policy sense, superior competence in planning and conducting negotiations, and a highly refined skill in oral and written expression.

A Career Minister is expected to have extensive knowledge of key governmental programs in the foreign affairs field. The Career Minister's perspective will encompass the complete range of considerations that are pertinent to foreign affairs decision making. The Career Minister's stature will have developed to the point where the officer's outlook is not colored or influenced by bureaucratic or parochial consideration, but is based upon a broad conceptual grasp of foreign policy.

The Career Minister will be not only a person knowledgeable in foreign affairs, but also one well versed in the current issues and problems of the American domestic scene. The officer may well have made a significant contribution to the Department of State's efforts to ensure that U.S. foreign policies have the understanding and support of the Congress and the American public.

Initiative rather than caution will have characterized the Career Minister's earlier career. The Career Minister's hallmark should be creative effort resulting in superlative achievement and occasional mistakes rather than an unquestioning adherence to the norm or precedent which produced an unblemished record of routinely bland or merely satisfactory performance. The Career Minister will have exhibited keen intellectual curiosity beyond the bounds of official business, and will have developed comprehension in depth of the political, economic and sociological forces at work in countries and areas to which the officer has been assigned. Blended with these qualities will be consistent evidence in the officer's performance of purposeful and effective effort to advance our national objectives.

The Career Minister will have shown a capacity to understand and deal effectively with foreign nationals in and out of government, and typically will have effective use of at least one foreign language.

The Career Minister should be capable of carrying out any assignment involving U.S. foreign affairs anywhere in the world. Promotion to the rank of Career Minister shall not be used as a reward for past performance; it will only be used as recognition of the clear promise to meet future challenges with extraordinary skill and dedication. It is, therefore, essential that Board I maintain unwaveringly these high qualifying standards.

Excerpts from the Foreign Service Act of 1980

SEC. 207. CHIEF OF MISSION.—(a) Under the direction of the President, the chief of mission to a foreign country—

(1) shall have full responsibility for the direction, coordination, and supervision of all Government employees in that country (except for employees under the command of a United States area military commander); and

(2) shall keep fully and currently informed with respect to all activities and operations of the Government within that country, and shall insure that all Government employees in that country (except for employees under the command of a United States area military commander) comply fully with all applicable directives of the chief of mission.

(b) Any agency having employees in a foreign country shall keep the chief of mission to that country fully and currently informed with respect to all activities and operations of its employees in that country, and shall insure that all of its employees in that country (except for employees under the command of a United States area military commander) comply fully with all applicable directives of the chief of mission.

SEC. 304. APPOINTMENT OF CHIEFS OF MISSION.—(a)(1) An individual appointed or assigned to be a chief of mission should possess clearly demonstrated competence to perform the duties of a chief of mission, including, to the maximum extent practicable, a useful knowledge of the principal language or dialect of the country in which the individual is to serve, and knowledge and understanding

From Public Law 96-465, 96th Congress, "An Act to promote the foreign policy of the United States by strengthening and improving the Foreign Service of the United States, and for other purposes," approved October 17, 1980, cited as "Foreign Service Act of 1980."

of the history, the culture, the economic and political institutions, and the interests of that country and its people.

(2) Given the qualifications specified in paragraph (1), positions as chief of mission should normally be accorded to career members of the Service, though circumstances will warrant appointments from time to time of qualified individuals who are not career members of the Service.

(3) Contributions to political campaigns should not be a factor in the appointment of an individual as a chief of mission.

(4) The President shall provide the Committee on Foreign Relations of the Senate, with each nomination for an appointment as a chief of mission, a report on the demonstrated competence of that nominee to perform the duties of the position in which he or she is to serve.

(b)(1) In order to assist the President in selecting qualified candidates for appointment or assignment as chiefs of mission, the Secretary of State shall from time to time furnish the President with the names of career members of the Service who are qualified to serve as chiefs of mission, together with pertinent information about such members.

(2) Each individual nominated by the President to be a chief of mission, ambassador at large, or minister shall, at the time of nomination, file with the Committee on Foreign Relations of the Senate and the Speaker of the House of Representatives a report of contributions made by such individual and by members of his or her immediate family during the period beginning on the first day of the fourth calendar year preceding the calendar year of the nomination and ending on the date of the nomination. The report shall be verified by the oath of the nominee, taken before any individual authorized to administer oaths. The chairman of the Committee on Foreign Relations of the Senate shall have each such report printed in the Congressional Record. As used in this paragraph, the term "contribution" has the same meaning given such term by section 301(8) of the Federal Election Campaign Act of 1971 (2 U.S.C. 431(8)), and the term "immediate family" means the spouse of the nominee, and any child, parent, grandparent, brother, or sister of the nominee and the spouses of any of them.

(c) Within 6 months after assuming the position, the chief of mission to a foreign country shall submit, to the Committee on Foreign Relations of the Senate and the Committee on Foreign

Affairs of the House of Representatives, a report describing his or her own foreign language competence and the foreign language competence of the mission staff in the principal language or other dialect of that country.

President Kennedy to Chiefs of Mission, May 29, 1961*

DEAR MR. AMBASSADOR: Please accept my best wishes for the successful accomplishment of your mission. As the personal representative of the President of the United States in. . . . you are part of a memorable tradition which began with Benjamin Franklin and Thomas Jefferson, and which has included many of our most distinguished citizens.

We are living in a critical moment in history. Powerful destructive forces are challenging the universal values which, for centuries, have inspired men of good will in all parts of the world.

If we are to make progress toward a prosperous community of nations in a world of peace, the United States must exercise the most affirmative and responsible leadership. Beyond our shores, this leadership, in large measure, must be provided by our ambassadors and their staffs.

I have asked you to represent our Government in. . . . because I am confident that you have the ability, dedication, and experience. The purpose of this letter is to define guidelines which I hope may be helpful to you.

The practice of modern diplomacy requires a close understanding not only of governments but also of people, their cultures and institutions. Therefore, I hope that you will plan your work so that you may have the time to travel extensively outside the nation's capital. Only in this way can you develop the close, personal associations that go beyond official diplomatic circles and maintain a sympathetic and accurate understanding of all segments of the country.

---

*Paragraphs 16 and 17 were omitted from the letters sent to Ambassadors in countries in which there were no United States military forces under an area military commander.

Moreover, the improved understanding which is so essential to a more peaceful and rational world is a two-way street. It is our task not only to understand what motivates others, but to give them a better understanding of what motivates us.

Many persons in. . . . who have never visited the United States, receive their principal impressions of our nation through their contact with Americans who come to their country either as private citizens or as government employees.

Therefore, the manner in which you and your staff personally conduct yourselves is of the utmost importance. This applies to the way in which you carry out your official duties and to the attitudes you and they bring to day-to-day contacts and associations.

It is an essential part of your task to create a climate of dignified, dedicated understanding, cooperation, and service in and around the Embassy.

In regard to your personal authority and responsibility, I shall count on you to oversee and coordinate all the activities of the United States Government in. . . .

You are in charge of the entire United States Diplomatic Mission, and I shall expect you to supervise all of its operations. The Mission includes not only the personnel of the Department of State and the Foreign Service, but also the representatives of all other United States agencies which have programs or activities in. . . . I shall give you full support and backing in carrying out your assignment.

Needless to say, the representatives of other agencies are expected to communicate directly with their offices here in Washington, and in the event of a decision by you in which they do not concur, they may ask to have the decision reviewed by a higher authority in Washington.

However, it is their responsibility to keep you fully informed of their views and activities and to abide by your decisions unless in some particular instance you and they are notified to the contrary.

If in your judgment individual members of the Mission are not functioning effectively, you should take whatever action you feel may be required, reporting the circumstances, of course, to the Department of State.

In case the departure from. . . . of any individual member of the Mission is indicated in your judgment, I shall expect you to make the decision and see that it is carried into effect. Such instances I am confident will be rare.

Now one word about your relations to the military. As you know, the United States Diplomatic Mission includes Service Attachés, Military Assistance Advisory Groups and other military components attached to the Mission. It does not, however, include United States military forces operating in the field where such forces are under the command of a United States area military commander. The line of authority to these forces runs from me, to the Secretary of Defense, to the Joint Chiefs of Staff in Washington and to the area commander in the field.

Although this means that the chief of the American Diplomatic Mission is not in the line of military command, nevertheless, as Chief of Mission, you should work closely with the appropriate area military commander to assure the full exchange of information. If it is your opinion that activities by the United States military forces may adversely affect our over-all relations with the people or government of . . . . , you should promptly discuss the matter with the military commander and, if necessary, request a decision by higher authority.

I have informed all heads of departments and agencies of the Government of the responsibilities of the chiefs of American Diplomatic Missions for our combined operations abroad, and I have asked them to instruct their representatives in the field accordingly.

As you know, your own lines of communication as Chief of Mission run through the Department of State.

Let me close with an expression of confidence in you personally and the earnest hope that your efforts may help strengthen our relations with both the Government and the people of. . . . I am sure that you will make a major contribution to the cause of world peace and understanding.

Good luck and my warmest regards,

Sincerely,

(Signed) JOHN F. KENNEDY

10

Cases in Point

Everybody agrees that it is better to have good ambassadors than bad ones. Everybody—or almost everybody—also agrees that there is really no foreign post nowadays that can be considered "unimportant." A few years ago El Salvador would have been regarded as a "safe" mission to entrust to an inexperienced ambassador. Cambodia was long regarded as an unimportant backwater until it became a key element in the Indochina conflict and the site of perhaps the greatest tragedy that any country has suffered in this century. Many a small and seemingly unimportant post can suddenly become of great importance to our national security.

The best ambassadors excel in performing the functions that have been enumerated and discussed. Some have become famous, a few even legendary. Often their status of eminence is attained through a long succession of small moves on the diplomatic checkerboard which are important only cumulatively as part of a larger picture.* Excellence is thus demonstrated over a period of time, by a consistently high batting average. Here we feature information on three successful ambassadors and two who did not work out. The cases we recall here have come to the public's attention. There have been and are of course many others.

Smith Simpson, a retired diplomat who served for over 20 years, is the author of *Anatomy of the State Department* (1967) and *The Crisis in American Diplomacy* (1980) from which a brief excerpt is reprinted here. **George Crile** is a free-lance writer whose article about Vincent de Roulet appeared in *Harper's*. **Winston Smith** was

---

*The Institute has analyzed a single telegram drafted by Ambassador David K. E. Bruce over thirty years ago which is a model of understated persuasiveness and complete command of a highly complex subject, in *David Bruce's "Long Telegram" of July 3, 1951* by Martin F. Herz. The telegram is credited with having precipitated an important change of approach in Washington to a problem of great importance.

the *nom de plume* chosen by Edward C. Ingraham, who was DCM (deputy chief of mission) to the unfortunate ambassador whose alleged weaknesses he decided to expose. His career was blighted by this whistle-blowing, and he has left the Foreign Service. **William H. Attwood,** a journalist, editor, and former publisher of *Newsday,* served as U.S. Ambassador to Guinea and to Kenya. We express our appreciation to Smith Simpson, the *Foreign Service Journal* and *Harper's* for permission to reprint.

Three Successful Diplomats

Smith Simpson

Because diplomacy is practiced across national, cultural, psychological and historical boundaries and even across different stages of civilization, it possesses an intellectual-cultural-psychological dimension which affects every function a diplomat performs. This is at the root of his problems of gathering and evaluating intelligence, reporting to his government thousands of miles and perhaps a whole historical period and civilization away, explaining his government's policies and the character of his nation, and performing his wide-ranging public relations work. It is a determinant of his ability to command respect from foreign nationals, as well as from his own, manage posts and programs intelligently, resolve conflicts and negotiate. It affects his role as a trade promoter, particularly in sophisticated societies. It affects not only his resourcefulness as a tactician but his ability to rise to the level of strategic thinking which in turn affects his competence to advise his government and the host government on policy issues.

It is this dimension which does much to explain the extraordinary capacities of the Benjamin Franklins, Thomas Jeffersons, Jules Jusserands, Lord Bryces, David Eugene Thompsons, Dwight Morrows, David K. E. Bruces, Ellsworth Bunkers, Chip Bohlens, Anatoly Dobrynins and all the other outstanding contributors to diplomacy. These have been men of unusual intellectual capacity, cultural breadth and depth and psychological insight.

Consider Jules Jusserand. He was the French ambassador in Washington for thirteen years, from 1903 to 1915, after having spent some years in the French diplomatic service in London, Constantinople and Copenhagen. Note, first, the length of service in Washington. Then take note of his publication in 1889 of a study of *English Wayfaring Life in the Middle Ages,* six years later a *Literary History of the English People* and in 1898 *Shakespeare in France.* If one is inclined to raise his eyebrows over the relevance of English wayfaring life in the middle ages or literary studies to 20th century

From *The Crisis in American Diplomacy* (West Hanover, MA: Christopher Publishing House, 1980), pp. 20–23. Reprinted by kind permission of the author.

diplomacy, he is betraying an ignorance of the cultural depth and subtleties demanded for diplomatic competence. He may be suggesting the very reason American diplomacy so seldom gets off the ground on the various continents of the world. And if he wonders how, today, a diplomatic officer of ours could possibly engage in such cultural pursuits, he may be raising one of the vital questions concering the quality of our diplomacy and our problem of world leadership which the American public, the President, the Congress and the State Department itself are failing to address.

Jusserand became a close friend and adviser of an American President, one generally considered so ebulliently self-confident as not to be in the market for much advice, especially from a foreigner. But when Theodore Roosevelt had a particularly difficult question to resolve, whether domestic or international, he came to seek the counsel of the French ambassador. When Secretary of State John Hay fell ill and the President wanted the best advice he could get on some foreign affairs question, he turned not to the Acting Secretary of State, nor to a member of his Cabinet, but to this learned, perceptive, personable emissary of France. Remarkable was this relationship and it could not have evolved from anything the French Government could have done save dispatch this exceptionally competent diplomat to Washington. Such influence could not have been exerted in Paris either by the President of France, her Premier or her Minister of Foreign Affairs, and any attempt to do so would have been brusquely rebuffed in Washington as "intervention" in American affairs. It could only be developed in the overseas capital itself by an erudite and empathic emissary. Here lies the subtle secret of influence and leadership in world affairs.

Since dictatorships are numerous these days, let us consider the mission of David Eugene Thompson. At a critical time in the history of Mexico, this Nebraskan was appointed our ambassador there. He was described by an American diplomatic officer who served with him as "a man of powerful personality, of large intelligence and shrewd judgment, and of sharp and forthright tongue. . . . By the lifelong exercise of a naturally strong intellect on a vast number and wide variety of books, he had, for all his lack of formal schooling, made himself into an unusually well-educated man. . . . His great value to his country lay in the fact that he possessed, as no other man possessed, the absolute confidence of the aging Mexican dictator, Don Porfirio Diaz . . . and the friendship between them illustrates the great and beneficent power a North American diplomat could, if he were trusted and well-liked, exercise unofficially in Spanish American capitals.'' Now observe what this produced: ''Aware of the relationship between the President and the Ambassador, State Governors, generals, police officials, federal judges and even judges of the supreme court would drop into the Embassy to consult him about any case that might happen to involve Americans or American interests.''

Here is influence—indirect, indeed, but effective all the same and indeed the greater because not exerted directly. It arose from respect. It therefore carried no taint of intervention. Is this not the secret of diplomacy? Is this not what diplomatic influence is all about? Is not this the kind of representative the United States should be sending abroad in all ranks of its diplomatic service—men and women of personality, large intelligence, culture, and shrewd judgment, people articulate, well-liked and trusted?

James Bryce, who served as the British Ambassador in Washington for six years (1907–13), although he had not held previously any diplomatic post, was well seasoned as a scholar, professor, party leader and government official, and had published a celebrated two-volume study of the United States, *The American Commonwealth*. His knowledge of the strengths and weaknesses of our society being profound, he was one of the most sentient and popular ambassadors ever to serve in this country. He was in great demand as a speaker and he spoke with typical British substance and grace. Wherever he went, he represented the best of British culture and did much, therefore, to nurture that pro-British sentiment which was to prove so useful to his government when the first of the world wars descended upon it. Here again, is not this the kind of favorable view and good will which the United States should be seeking throughout the world by sending its best people to represent it? What does it gain by sending second- and third-rate people and even clowns?

Our Man in Jamaica

George Crile

To say that Vincent de Roulet was the worst Ambassador in the
annals of American diplomacy is perhaps to overstate the matter
(he was, after all, responsible for no invasions or civil insurrections),
but to say that he was an unreliable amateur seems to me a fair
comment on a record that needs only a few words of introduction.
Although he had been the American Ambassador in Jamaica from
1969 to 1973, few people had heard of him until the occasion of his
public disgrace. Declared persona non grata by the Jamaican government in July 1973, de Roulet was heard to describe the Prime
Minister of that government as "an emotional Yo-Yo." Few diplomats speak in such plain words, and so I was surprised that the
American press gave only brief notice to de Roulet's dismissal. No
matter how careless their deportment or how profound their stupid-
ity, American Ambassadors seldom get sent home, particularly
from small and dependent countries in the so-called Third World. I
assumed that there was more to the story than a few paragraphs on
an inside page of the *Times*. Preliminary inquiries among friends at
the State Department suggested so strange a chronicle of folly and
embarrassment that I left immediately for Kingston. I was amazed
to find that even in remote Jamaican villages there were people who
remembered de Roulet's name with derisive laughter.

Still unwilling to believe what I had been told, I returned to New
York to talk to de Roulet himself. He had been described to me as
an "aggressively arrogant" man who took pride in his "forthright
and pithy" manner of address. He was said to be brooding in his
apartment on Fifth Avenue, and, if my information was correct, I
reasoned that he would be anxious to tell his side of the story, to
rescue his reputation from what I was sure he would regard as the
calumny of his social inferiors. In this I was not disappointed.

De Roulet granted me two audiences, on one occasion allowing
me to transcribe his remarks on a tape recorder. Throughout both
conversations he maintained an attitude of sublime confidence, as
if assured that one day the injustice done to him by lesser men

would be understood in its proper light. Well over six feet, de Roulet spoke with an impetuous haste that I learned to recognize as consistent with his idea of himself as a man of action.

The following narrative relies largely on de Roulet's own recollection of the events that led to his expulsion from Jamaica. The more implausible episodes in the narrative I subsequently verified (and sometimes amplified) by talking to correspondents in Jamaica

---

They Got the Message

The story is still told of the American ambassador in a country to the south who received instructions from Washington to make representations in the strongest possible terms to obtain extradition of a narcotics smuggler who had apparently bought himself protection there with his ill-gotten riches.

Concerned that the relations of easy informality and trust which he had established with the country's leadership should not suffer, the ambassador made his *démarche* but gave Washington no evidence that he had done so with the vigor and urgency that had been requested in his instructions. He then was given new instructions to raise the subject to the highest level and make clear that it went to the heart of the country's relationship with the United States.

The ambassador, apparently disbelieving his instructions or convinced that the matter did not warrant using such strong language, or embarrassed to use strong language, reported back the evasive responses, obfuscations and dilatory maneuvers of the local government, with some evidence in his message to Washington that he did not feel the issue merited pulling out all the stops and that he had therefore not done so.

He was thereupon summarily fired by Washington (he was a career officer); and it was the withdrawal of the American ambassador which finally convinced the local government that the United States meant business.

—M.F.H.

---

and officials in the State Department. I have tried to present the Ambassador's point of view, and I do not mean to detract from what he considers to be his considerable accomplishment. . . .

Although willing to consider any form of government service, de Roulet felt that he would be most useful as an Ambassador. At the age of 42 he was a rich man, unashamedly proud of his race horses, his yacht, his clubs, his inherited wealth. He sometimes boasted that he had been born into money, and that his wife—"a Whitney, you know"—belonged to one of the richest families in the country. He believed in the idea of what he called "a certain noblesse oblige in us."

De Roulet was a political conservative and would, no doubt, have contributed generously to Richard Nixon's Presidential campaign regardless of his ambitions. But, having made the decision to invest in the campaign, he thought seriously about exploring the opportunities available to him in a Nixon administration. For the first time in his life he sat down to write his curriculum vitae. . . .

Having decided on a government career, de Roulet had to find out how to get an appointment appropriate for a man of his background and experience. "I wanted to deal with the right guy," he said. "I didn't want to go through seventeen committees and all this, that, and the other thing." One option open to him was to inquire of H. R. Haldeman. De Roulet's father had introduced Haldeman's parents to each other, and the two boys had grown up together in Los Angeles, but for the task at hand he sought out another old California friend—a Republican fund raiser who set up a meeting for de Roulet with Maurice Stans.

De Roulet resented the suggestion that he sought to purchase an Ambassadorship. "They've never proved any Ambassadorships were for sale. In fact, Stans specifically told me at our first meeting that Ambassadorships are not for sale at any price." In any event, after the meeting, de Roulet said he spoke to his wife and then decided to contribute $50,000 to the 1968 campaign; a few months later he "ponied up" another $25,000, and shortly after the election he was appointed United States Ambassador to Jamaica.*

In October 1969 de Roulet arrived at Kingston aboard his ninety-foot yacht, *Patrina*. Together with a stable of race horses that he intended to run at the Cayman track, he brought with him his amateur's conviction that many Foreign Service officers weren't up to the challenge of true diplomacy. Within a few weeks of his arrival he developed a new respect for the complexity of his mission.

"Everybody thinks of Jamaica as an island in the sun where you drink rum and copulate with octoroons," he said, "but I can tell you it's rough as hell. I jumped to my gun all the time. I even carried a gun in my lap when we drove through Kingston.". . .

Outside of the embassy, the new Ambassador quickly demonstrated a talent for offending the sensibilities of his host country. In his conversations with me he spoke of the Jamaicans as "the most

---

*All told, de Roulet and his wife contributed $175,000 to the two Nixon campaigns. De Roulet's mother-in-law, Mrs. Joan Whitney Payson, was also a major contributor—$113,000 to the two Nixon campaigns, as well as $83,000 to Republican Congressional candidates.

spoiled race of people in the world," as "idiots," and as people suffering from a "rampant inferiority complex." During his tenure as Ambassador his public characterizations were even less flattering. He casually referred to Jamaicans as "children," and in *Time* magazine he was reported to have called them "niggers." He apparently didn't think that he was offending anyone. Neither did he think it impolitic to remark, as he frequently did, that Jamaica offered less for the tourist dollar than any other resort with which he was familiar. . . .

Although de Roulet's idea of diplomacy often seemed to lead to trouble, it was, at least in the beginning, also responsible for a remarkable success. This came in the key area of diplomatic concern in Jamaica—the status of approximately $650 million worth of bauxite holdings owned by five American aluminum companies— Alcoa, Revere, Kaiser, Reynolds, and Anaconda. The importance of these holdings is substantial; aluminum is made from bauxite, and the United States relies on Jamaica for 60 percent of its imports. The State Department, wary of de Roulet's inexperience, instructed the new Ambassador to avoid any dealings with either the Jamaican government or the American aluminum companies over the bauxite question. The prohibition had a perverse effect on de Roulet; he made bauxite his consuming preoccupation. When he spoke of his efforts in this area, he did so with pride.

His first contact with the issue came immediately upon his arrival in Jamaica. The federal government, through its Overseas Private Investment Corporation (OPIC), had already extended $300 million worth of loan guarantees on U.S. bauxite/alumina investments in Jamaica, and it was recommending increasing that amount to $500 million. All·that remained for the new guarantees to go through was for the new Ambassador to grant his approval; it was considered a mere formality. De Roulet, however, surprised everyone by first refusing and then steadfastly resisting pressures to grant his approval. He said the risk to the United States was too great; in his opinion the American aluminum companies had been irresponsible citizens in Jamaica, and he believed that nationalization or expropriation had become a distinct possibility.

For six months, de Roulet held up the loan guarantees. Finally, he gave his approval but only after receiving assurances from OPIC that no more loan guarantees would be issued in Jamaica. The Ambassador didn't approve of the OPIC program—but once the

$500 million in loan guarantees had been issued, he considered it his responsibility to do whatever was necessary to protect the financial interests of his government. If that included disobeying the orders of his State Department supervisors, so be it. "There are certain things a freewheeling guy with lots of money can do," he explained. "I don't have to worry about being sent back to Washington to live in a split-level house in suburbia for the rest of my life."

What ensued was a campaign of unconventional diplomacy in which a Senate subcommittee later found that de Roulet had resorted to special favors and implied threats in order to accomplish the objective he had been specifically instructed not to pursue. He had begun by browbeating the chief executives of the American aluminum companies—insisting that they see to it that their companies improve their public standing in Jamaica.

These companies had come to Jamaica in the early 1950s; they bought up thousands of acres of land, scattering thousands of farm families into the country's overcrowded cities. The Jamaicans received little in return because the American firms succeeded in writing agreements that allowed them to pay minimal taxes despite the enormity of their investments. Further, the mining process, roughly the equivalent of strip mining, employs relatively few workers and devastates the landscape. . . .

Until his intervention the chief executives of the aluminum companies had never directly involved themselves with their companies' affairs in Jamaica. But at de Roulet's insistence these executives flew to Jamaica for at least ten meetings with the Jamaican government. As a result, the companies began to seriously support social programs in the country. Encouraged by this success, de Roulet began to extend his interventions into Jamaican politics. An election was coming up, and de Roulet set out to keep the question of nationalization of the American bauxite companies from being introduced into the campaign debate. He wasn't worried about the incumbent Prime Minister, Hugh Shearer, for the two men were friends. Shearer was what de Roulet called a "realist"—that is, a man willing to strike a deal. "In the whole time I dealt with him," de Roulet said, "I never had to listen to a long speech about his little people with withering bellies and the back-to-Africa crap. He was a hard-boiled businessman. He knew where his bread was buttered."

De Roulet was worried, however, about Shearer's rival in the election, Michael Manley. The danger with Manley, he explained, was that "he was much more of a socialist dedicated to an egalitarian society." De Roulet felt it essential to the interests of the United States to keep Manley from taking office, and he devised what was later characterized as a "deal" to get Shearer reelected. . . .

"De Roulet did not understand why the Assistant Secretary was getting so excited. . . . It seemed too him that Hurwitch was making a mountain out of a molehill. It seemed that everybody was. Within a matter of hours, Prime Minister Manley had taken the drastic step of declaring him persona non grata, and overnight the incident was transformed into a large national controversy, known in the Jamaican papers as the 'de Roulet Affair.' De Roulet reasoned that Manley's actions were the product of a psychologically troubled mind."

It was a few months later, in the spring of 1971, that de Roulet reached the zenith of his brief career in the Foreign Service. He had violated virtually every diplomatic taboo, but none of that seemed to matter. He was a success. Not a humdrum success, mind you, but a full-blown, officially certified success. The declaration was made by a team of career Foreign Service officers in a confidential inspection report which begins as follows: "Under the vigorous, skillful, and intelligent leadership of a non-career Chief of Mission, Embassy Kingston gets highest marks for its achievements with respect to US objectives." The inspectors commented that the Ambassador's diplomatic style was unconventional, but, they concluded, "It works."

Also at about this time, President Nixon's personal lawyer, Herbert Kalmbach, flew to Jamaica to attend Mrs. de Roulet's birthday party. The Ambassador pledged Kalmbach $400,000 for the President's 1972 campaign. De Roulet had begun to dream of an ambassadorial assignment in Europe. The next year, however, his candidate for Prime Minister unfortunately lost the election. Instead of Hugh Shearer, the Jamaican electorate chose Michael Manley, the son of one of Jamaica's national heroes and himself a deeply popular and charismatic leader. . . .

[De Roulet] was suspicious of Manley, suspicious of him despite his polished manners and education at the London School of Economics. Among the people in Manley's government de Roulet saw only a pitiful parallel to the kinds of government officials found in postcolonial Africa. "You know," he said, "somebody once said that every one of those cute little countries always got a guy who was twenty-eight years old from the London School of Economics as Finance Minister, and it's so true. It's sooooo true.". . .

Aside from an occasional minor incident, de Roulet subsided into boredom and torpor as he awaited news on his expected promotion. In the meantime, he turned his attentions to his race horses and contented himself with making friends with John Connally, then in Jamaica trying to work out a cattle deal with the Manley government. Occasionally de Roulet roused himself to his old form. On one such occasion, he delivered a lecture to a mixed audience of Americans and Jamaicans in which he declared that Prime Minister Manley had an ambivalent personality, which he attributed to Manley's mixed racial origin. But none of this got him into any serious trouble until he was called back to Washington to testify before a Senate subcommittee investigating the abuses of multinational corporations. He was asked to comment on any actions he might have taken to protect US bauxite investments in Jamaica. To the surprise of his audience of Senators, de Roulet freely described what he had done to get Shearer's assurance not to raise the issue of nationalization. And then he dropped his bombshell. He said that he had managed to extract a similar promise from Michael Manley during the elections. The Ambassador explained that Manley and his advisers were fearful that the CIA might intervene in the Jamaican elections as it had allegedly done several years before in Guyana. In his testimony, de Roulet said he had taken advantage of the situation by offering Manley his word "as a gentleman" that the United States would not interfere in the coming election. In return, de Roulet said, he asked for and won a pledge from Manley not to raise the nationalization issue in the campaign.

The State Department was dumbfounded. Ambassadors are not supposed to do that sort of thing, and if they do they're certainly not supposed to talk about it—at least not in public. The Acting Assistant Secretary of State for Inter-American Affairs, Robert Hurwitch, immediately asked for the opportunity to set the record straight. He was worried that the impression might have been left that the State Department had been a party to some sort of improper "deals." Hurwitch acknowledged that prior to 1969 the United States had dealt with other countries in the hemisphere "as client states or with some kind of patronizing attitude," but all that has changed, he insisted. No longer was the United States employing what he called "trashy tactics." Hurwitch pleaded for understanding. "There is no deal, was no deal, nor was any deal intended," he told the now-astounded Senators. And then he made a similar appeal to the press and to any members of the embassy of Jamaica who might be present. They must understand and make their countrymen understand "that there was no intervention by the United States, past, present, or future, none was planned, and there was no deal on this matter."*

De Roulet, who was listening as Hurwitch spoke, did not understand why the Assistant Secretary was getting so excited. "I think it's perfectly proper to solicit something out of a politician when he's running for office," he observed later. It seemed to him that Hurwitch was making a bit of a mountain out of a molehill. It seemed that everyone was. Within a matter of hours, Prime Minister Manley had taken the drastic step of declaring him persona non grata, and overnight the incident was transformed into a raging national controversy, known in the Jamaican papers as the "de Roulet Affair." De Roulet reasoned that Manley's actions were the product of a psychologically troubled man. . . .

The Ambassador then reflected on the special virtues he had brought to his job. "Linda comes from the Whitney family, whom I'm sure you've heard of, and my family had some money. You've got a certain noblesse oblige in us. That's really what it was all about—noblesse oblige—but it was a noblesse oblige with an activist zeal."

De Roulet's only real regret is that he might not have a chance to put his ability to work elsewhere. "I wanted to go where there was excitement, wheeling and dealing, where I could put to use the things I'd learned in Jamaica."

---

*Until de Roulet's testimony, the only public calls in Jamaica for nationalization of the bauxite industry had come from a few left-wing professors at Jamaica's universities. But thereafter no serious Jamaican politician could afford to be known as a toady of the United States. Within months, the Jamaicans, following the lead of the Arab oil countries, tripled the taxes and royalties taken from the American aluminum companies. Most knowledgeable observers believe this is only the first in a series of planned moves.

When we walked out of the Links Club, we stepped into his dark limousine and he stretched out his legs as his chauffeur pulled away from the curb and turned down Park Avenue. The Ambassador suddenly gestured to the apartment buildings on his left and right and spoke with a restored note of conviction: "I know people all around here and all they do is complain all the time. Well, I went out and did something about it."

Political Appointee: A Case Study

Winston Smith

We were at an evening social function. The ambassador and I were standing in a corner of the terrace, talking to a senior official of the host government who was anxious to tell us about his just-concluded visit to the United States. He had been asked by a neighboring government to sound out American officials on a del-icate subject during the visit, and he began to describe to us the outcome of his inquiries. The ambassador, a political appointee, couldn't follow the conversation. At the first opportunity, he broke in to ask genially, "Did you get in any golf while you were in the States?"

Rewarding a political supporter by naming him ambassador to a salubrious foreign capital is a practice as old as the Republic. Although a uniquely American product, it has not been one of our more felicitous political traditions. Mention of political appointees is apt to invoke memories: the envoy to Sri Lanka who gained fleeting fame by admitting that he did not know the name of his host coun-try's prime minister; the ambassador to a Latin American country who adamantly refused to let the embassy staff operate out of his undamaged residence after the chancery had been demolished in an earthquake; the businessman-turned-diplomat who solemnly explained that former Dominican dictator Trujillo was really a fine man led astray by evil companions and advisers. These, of course, are all images from the past. What about the present?

A recent assignment has induced me to take a new look at this hoary institution and how it has been faring under the present administration. The experience was far from unique but it did pro-vide the occasion for a good deal of reflection on the problem of the political appointee, some of which I would like to share with you.

Although there has been a tendency on the part of career officers to see the term "political appointee" as synonymous with "non-career appointee," an important distinction can be made between

Reprinted, in condensed form, by permission from the *Foreign Service Journal*, January 1980.

them. From the very beginning, US administrations have routinely reached outside the ranks of government to appoint private citizens of demonstrated ability and often distinguished records to ambassadorial positions. Indeed, until World War II most of our chiefs of mission came from this source. Among contemporary examples of such appointments one can cite Ambassador Mansfield in Tokyo, Ambassador Goheen in New Delhi and Ambassador Wriggins in Colombo, persons whose selection as chiefs of mission even the most career-minded of foreign service professionals can hardly criticize. All appointments of this nature may not have been equally worthy, but they have rarely been a valid source of discontent to the professionals. . . .

But appointments of this sort are not really what we mean when we talk about "political appointees." If one sets aside the university presidents, scholars, retired legislators and civic-minded philanthropists whose appointments—although motivated in good part by political considerations—can be seen as at least reasonably appropriate to the job, we are left with a residue of other non-career appointees. These are the ones who have no visible qualifications for the position and nothing in their backgrounds to suggest any particular affinity for foreign affairs. They are the true political appointees, those who have obviously been selected for reasons that have nothing to do with the conduct of foreign policy. It is primarily from this group that the diplomatic horror stories of the past have come. . . .

None of the embassy staff had ever laid eyes on Ambassador X when we assembled at the airport to meet him on his arrival at the post. Our initial impressions were favorable. During our first few minutes of conversation he seemed friendly, unassuming, alert, crisp and not overly taken with his own importance. My first misgivings arose when we rode together into the city from the airport. Although he had never before been in that part of the world and the route passed through some especially interesting parts of the city, I noticed that he did not once glance out the window at his new surroundings. Nor did he ask any questions about the country. He spent the time talking about the important people he had met in Washington and at a stop-over en route.

Ambassador X's first days in office were unexceptional, devoted largely to meeting the staff, leafing through the briefing material we had prepared for him, listening to a series of oral briefings, and familiarizing himself with the office layout. At the same time, he began reading the incoming cable traffic. The first sign of anything unusual came about a week after his arrival, when one of the secretaries emerged wide-eyed from his office, rushed over to me and said, "He just asked me where Canberra was!"

This was the modest beginning of our progressive exposure to Ambassador X's fund of information. In short order senior staff members were presented with, among many others, the following questions:

"What is this 'gang of four' that everyone is talking about?"

"You mean there has been a war between India and Pakistan? What was that all about?"

"Did you say there are two separate Korean governments? How come?"

Among people he had never heard of, we found, were Gandhi, Nehru, Sukarno, former British Prime Minister Callahan (then still in office), Chancellor Schmidt and Chiang Kai-shek, to say nothing of such nonentities as Deng Xiaoping and President Giscard d'Estaing. Even more startling was a conversation with several fellow chiefs of mission in a neighboring capital some months later. The discussion turned to the resurgence of Islam and its possible impact on the region; at that point, Ambassador X asked, "What's Islam?"

This mind-boggling lack of information was by no means confined to the foreign policy field. At one unforgettable staff meeting, Ambassador X opened the proceedings by complaining of his lingering cold and wondering aloud whether he should send someone out to buy him "some antibiotics." He acted surprised when a staff member observed that a doctor's prescription would be necessary, and showed incomprehension when another suggested that an antihistamine ("a *what?*") would be more effective. He became animated when a third staff member extolled the virtues of Vitamin C and offered to give him a supply. "It's not habit-forming, is it?" he asked nervously. . . .

Meanwhile, as the depth of his information gap was being plumbed, other traits were emerging. One concerned his personal work habits. During his first weeks in office, we attributed to delayed jet lag his failure to return to the office after going home for an early lunch. We later found, however, that this was simply his style. Out of curiosity I once checked the Marine Guard logbook that recorded all his comings and goings; over a three-month period he had averaged slightly less than 21 hours a week in the office.

Ambassador X also did not write—at first almost literally. . . . He eventually did make an effort to draft a few messages. The first products were wholly embarrassing, but I thought I could detect signs of progressive improvement. He would never be a drafting officer, but he did show promise of becoming able to express himself coherently once the reader got past his stylistic quirks. I fancied that I was helping him in the process.

"Among people he had never heard of, we found, were Gandhi, Nehru, Sukarno, former British Prime Minister Callahan (then still in office), Chancellor Schmidt, Chiang Kai-shek, to say nothing of such nonentities as Deng Xiaoping and President Giscard d'Estaing. Even more startling was a conversation with several fellow chiefs of mission in a neighboring capital some months later. The discussion turned to the resurgence of Islam and its possible impact on the region; at that point Ambassador X asked, 'What's Islam?' "

A more serious problem arose in our efforts to develop local contacts for Ambassador X and to introduce him into the active intellectual/representational life of the capital. Shortly after he arrived, we persuaded him to host a large two-part reception at the residence for senior host country officials, the diplomatic corps and leading local citizens. With that successfully behind us, I suggested a few weeks later that we sit down and work out a representational program for him. Absolutely not. He and his wife heartily disliked entertaining, he said emphatically. One of the reasons they had taken an ambassadorship rather than a Washington appointment, he declared, was their fear of the heavy social schedule that the latter might entail! . . .

After initially balking. Ambassador X did dutifully attend most of the endless round of national day celebrations, receptions, dinner parties, and similar events that consume so much of a chief of mission's time. His sense of propriety was not very well developed, however, and he really didn't listen to our earnest lectures on local social customs, so odd incidents occurred. His seat of honor would be glaringly empty after the intermission at a concert, and he once innocently walked out of a ceremony minutes before the deputy prime minister rose to officiate, leaving both the DPM and the diplomatic corps openmouthed.

I recall most vividly one occasion when he was called upon to escort a party of senior officials, including the brigadier commanding a third-country military installation, on a tour of a visiting American warship. Halfway through the tour he abandoned them so that he could join his own household, which had just arrived at the ship for a separate tour. I still puzzle over just what happened next, but I remember well the vignette in the admiral's cabin a half hour later when the rest of the party had finished the tour and was waiting for the ambassador. Standing around a table were a permanent secretary, several senior host country military officers, the brigadier, myself, and one other host country citizen whom I knew only too well, acting as impromptu host to the permanent secretary. The brigadier turned to me and whispered, "Who is the gentleman talking to the permanent secretary?"

Taking a deep breath, I replied, "Oh, that's the ambassador's houseboy."

Ambassador X had dispatched the houseboy as a stand-in until he himself was able to rejoin the party. The brigadier did not say a word but I will not forget the look of frozen horror on his face.

There were a host of other oddities. Personal friends from home would visit Ambassador X at the residence, sometimes settling in for weeks on end. He would drop everything to entertain them, never an easy task for him since he had not identified, let alone visited, any of the capital's main tourist attractions. To pass the time, he would bring them to his office to sit, often for hours, while he conducted . . . business in front of them. One day I found to my alarm that one of them was actually sitting in on a rather highly classified country team meeting. Ambassador X did not take kindly to my subsequent suggestion that this was not a good idea (it brought forth his first accusation of "disloyalty") but he did get the message.

Ambassador X is the stuff from which Foreign Service legends are made, and I could go on in this vein almost indefinitely. My purpose in this article, however, is not to entertain the reader or to ridicule Ambassador X. He is, to repeat, a decent man, although entirely unqualified for the job he holds. That such a person has been appointed ambassador, as we all know, is by no means a rarity. There have been far worse ambassadorial appointments in the past few decades, although I doubt that any have arrived at their posts bearing as little knowledge of the outside world as he. What bothered me most about Ambassador X was that this administration was supposed to be different. We had the president's campaign promise, we had the Askew Committee—I suppose it was naive to feel a bit cheated.

My own involvement with Ambassador X ended abruptly after eight months, when he determined to replace me as DCM. We had both made a sincere effort to work together, but the strain proved too much for him. He found his new position increasingly frustrating as the divergence between his particular talents and the requirements of the job became ever more apparent to him. The frustration inevitably focused on his DCM, the one person always present at his humiliations and the one with the unwelcome but unavoidable task of constantly explaining to him why he could not do something he wanted to do and vice versa. I thought for a while that we had worked out a satisfactory modus vivendi, but I was mistaken.

As with most of his activities, Ambassador X's method of relieving me was unorthodox. Rather than telling me to my face that he was replacing me, he thrust a letter into my hand one morning, grabbed his expensive briefcase and strode rapidly out of the office, not to return until the following day.

The letter was a long one, explaining in painful detail why he considered the step necessary. The language was stiff and archaic, but it made his points graphically. Having no inkling that the letter was coming, my immediate reaction was one of surprise. Beneath the surprise, however, was an odd, niggling feeling of accomplishment. It was by far the best thing he had ever written! . . .

The Case Study

[Letter to the *Foreign Service Journal*]

The "case study" of a politically appointed ambassador in your January issue by the anonymous author with the Orwellian pseudonym "Winston Smith" perpetuates the hoary myth that all chiefs of mission who didn't shoulder their way up the FSO ladder have been bumbling dolts frustrating the legitimate ambitions of our skilled and sensitive corps of professional foreign service officers.

Well, I accepted three ambassadorial appointments during the Kennedy and Johnson administrations and I met a lot of dedicated, talented men and women and also a fair number of stuffed shirts and damned fools. And the latter included both career people and politicals.

In retrospect and on balance, I'd say the Foreign Service is fortunate to have an infusion of what we then called "non-career professionals" from time to time if only to stir up the bureaucracy, question outdated policies and write messages that don't all start with the classic, self-protecting "while."

Clearly, no one should be appointed who isn't at least as well qualified as the average career ambassador. But that's not too hard. Thinking of some of the "political" ambassadors who were my colleagues from 1961 to 1966—John Bartlow Martin, Ed Reischauer, Phil Kaiser, Lincoln Gordon, Bill Mahoney, Adlai Stevenson, Carl Rowan, Chester Bowles, Jim Loeb, Ken Galbraith, Bill Blair, Bob Good and so many others—I suspect that the officers who served with them would not compare them unfavorably with their career counterparts.

That's why I find the "Winston Smith" article both gratuitous and irresponsible—even if this extraordinary case he describes could be accepted as factual.

WILLIAM ATTWOOD

New Canaan, Conn.

Reprinted from "Letters," *Foreign Service Journal*, March 1980.

Concluding Observations

Elliot L. Richardson

If problems were fish, they would be easy to count. We could also measure them and sort them in accordance with weight, length, girth, color, number of dorsal rays, and so on. With a bit of effort, we might even derive a common unit of "fishiness."

Problems aren't fish, to be sure. Yet it is intriguing to speculate about the insights to be gained from the formulation—or at least the supposition—of a constant that would enable us to gauge the extent to which the problems facing today's world differ in scale and complexity from those confronted by our forebears. Ways of using such a constant come readily to mind. We might, for example, undertake to quantify the demands on American diplomats at, say, thirty-year intervals from 1790 to 1940 and ten-year intervals since then. The resulting comparisons would shed considerable light on the issues discussed in this volume. I hope that some ambitious graduate student will rise to the bait: dissertations have been elaborated around theses far less interesting. Meanwhile, we can at least make some educated guesses as to what the figures would show.

It's a good bet, for instance, that for most of the time between 1800 and 1910 the trend lines would be relatively flat. Three sharp spikes would identify the years in which wars occurred, but in most of our overseas posts during most of the period the crisis of the year would be a dispute over a letter of credit or the killing of an American seaman in a waterfront brawl. Indeed, it is likely that Charles Francis Adams' Civil War tour in London was the first American diplomatic mission to demand extraordinary judgment and skill since Franklin, Jefferson, and Charles' grandfather John represented the infant Republic in the capitals of Europe.

The World War I numbers, as in the case of previous wars, would show an abrupt climb, with the difference that after the war, instead

Elliot L. Richardson was United States Ambassador to Great Britain. He has held four cabinet positions: Secretary of Health, Education and Welfare; Secretary of Defense; Attorney General; and Secretary of Commerce. He served as Under Secretary of State (then the number two position) and as Special Representative to the Law of the Sea Conference with rank of ambassador. He is at present partner in a Washington law firm.

of falling all the way back to their earlier level, they would begin to reflect greater U.S. involvement with and interest in the rest of the world. But not until after World War II would U.S. diplomatic activity correspond to the nation's power, responsibility, and capacity for initiative. After Vietnam and Watergate, a new set of problems would begin to be generated by the growing gap between the aggregate demands of our external interests and the resources available for their protection and advancement. The principal contributors to the emergence of this gap would be declines in the political utility of the available carrots and sticks. Military power had depreciated in political value as the consequence both of the growing reluctance of public opinion to contemplate its use and of its virtually total absorption in the task of keeping strategic stalemates firmly locked into place.* Politically disposable economic power had diminished as the result of shrinkage in the relative U.S. share of world production and a quantum jump in the capability of our competitors.

New technology coupled with a vast expansion of worldwide trade and investment was meanwhile creating an ever more elaborate and widely ramified web of economic interconnections. The complexity thereby generated was compounded again by the necessity for coping with the systemic relationships among these interconnections. The increasing importance to the U.S. economy of imports, exports, foreign direct investment, and overseas lending forced international economic issues to the top of our domestic agenda, thereby blurring the traditional lines between foreign and domestic policy and exposing inadequacies in our policy-making machinery that still await correction. The concurrent increase in the necessity for addressing such issues in a multilateral context has not yet been matched by a comparable increase in our capacity to do so.

In addition to demonstrating the explosive growth in the demands on the nation's foreign policy resources, the periodic comparisons would also reveal that an increasing share of responsibility for meeting these demands has had to be delegated. Not even for the benefit of Presidents and Secretaries of State has modern technology found a way to lengthen the day, nor has science yet been able

---

*The latter process has, of course, diminished the political utility of Soviet military power no less than our own.

to sharpen their thought processes, multiply their energy, or improve their memory. In their struggle to cope with the volume and complexity of the claims on their attention, their only recourse has been to expand their staffs, but this has not precluded the necessity for pushing downward and outward into the system whole categories of problems that would once have landed on their desks.

Our quantitative comparisons would tell us what has been happening. Assuming that Q is a quantum reflecting importance, difficulty, and political sensitivity, we could see, for example, that until 1940 any foreign-policy problem with a magnitude of 10 Q or above invariably came before the Secretary of State; we could also see that he has time these days only for matters with magnitudes of 25 Q and above. The 10 Q problems, of course, are no easier than they used to be; the difference is that they now have to be handled by country directors and ambassadors.

"But the contributions of a good ambassador are not limited to the persuasive articulation and skillful execution of administration policy, good or bad. What he (or she) reports and how he reports it; the astuteness of his recommendations; his willingness to take the initiative; the courage to disagree and explain why—these and many other attributes can make a vital difference to the shaping of policy. How much depends on the good sense of his principals."

An incidental consequence of this quantitative exercise would be the demise of the simplistic notion that the rapidity of modern communications has downgraded the ambassador's role. It would demonstrate instead that most of what the telegraph and telephone could do to bring chiefs of mission under the more direct control of their home offices has long since been accomplished; it would likewise make clear that the technological improvements achieved in the last decade or two have done little or nothing to offset the added burdens thrust upon ambassadors.

In the absence of such incontrovertible data, the impression survives that ambassadors are merely glorified messenger boys. This weary canard has all too often, especially of late, encouraged the appointing authorities to slight the task of selecting individuals with the requisite quality and qualifications. Ambassadors' staff support and representational allowances have been squeezed down at a time when the requirements of the job should have led to the opposite result. Not so much by design as by inadvertence, repeated blows have been delivered to the morale of the career Foreign Service officers upon whom every State Department bureau and overseas mission, without regard to the career or non-career status of its head, must depend.

To recapitulate, our quantitative analysis would establish that during the past two decades U.S. global responsibilities have not diminished but, if anything, increased; that during this period there has been a relative decline in U.S. power to meet these responsibilities; that the aggregate volume, difficulty, and complexity of our foreign-policy problems have grown as the combined result both of this decline and of the growth in global interdependence; and that the corresponding increase in the responsibilities thrust upon our diplomatic establishment has not been offset by a comparable increase in its capacity to handle them.

It is not surprising in the circumstances that U.S. prestige, influence, and leadership have already started on a downward path. Assuming that we are not prepared to relax and enjoy the Spenglerian implications of this incipient trend, we have no choice but to embark on a sustained effort to counteract the relative decline in our disposable power by finding ways to husband our foreign policy resources more carefully and deploy them more efficiently. This will require synergism among four related measures: first, pruning and sharpening the definitions of our enduring interests; second, creating a coherent conceptual and strategic framework for a steady and consistent foreign policy; third, rebuilding the public consensus necessary to sustain this framework; and, fourth, strengthening the capacity of our diplomatic establishment to carry out its manifold functions with greater finesse.

It is the last of these measures that most directly concerns us here. How successfully it can be carried out will largely depend on the quality of U.S. representation abroad. This is not to say, of course, that good diplomacy can make up for bad policy. The maxim "garbage in, garbage out" has scarcely less application to diplomacy than to computers; indeed, the only obvious difference is that competent diplomacy can mask the odor. But the contributions of a good ambassador are not limited to the persuasive articulation and skillful execution of administration policy, good or bad. What he (or she) reports and how he reports it; the astuteness of his recommendations; his willingness to take the initiative; the courage to disagree and explain why—these and many other attributes can make a vital difference to the shaping of policy. How much difference depends on the good sense of his principals.

At its best, the relationship between the political leadership and career professionals is mutually reinforcing. Only the former can make the ultimate political choices, but they are foolish to do so without taking full advantage of the knowledge, experience, and skill of their professional colleagues. The latter, having done all they can to make sure that the decision-making process has intelligently taken their input into account, are chargeable (questions of conscience aside) with doing their best to give effect to the outcome. And just as the political leadership should be willing to fight for foreign policy objectives that must on occasion be given priority over domestic political concerns, so the career professional should be sensitive to the situations in which it is legitimate to let such concerns influence foreign policy judgments.

Properly understood on both sides, the relationship will develop a foundation of mutual respect and give rise to reciprocal trust. Where these elements are not present, the nation's foreign affairs cannot be conducted with the wisdom that the national interest requires. Where they come together, the national interest prospers. We have greater need than ever to reinforce this convergence.